How To Invest In Stocks

Completely revised second edition

V. SUBHASH

A plain-English guide to investing in the stockmarket

How To Invest In Stocks
2nd Edition

Written and designed by

V. Subhash

Copyright

© 2021 V. Subhash. All rights reserved.

Published and printed by

V. Subhash (www.VSubhash.in)
(First edition published in 2003. Second edition published in 2021.)

Disclaimer

Because prominent Wall Street firms have been caught betting against their clients (and still getting away with it), giving financial advice has become a serious thing. For this reason, it is stated that the author of this book is not authorised or certified by any accredited financial or educational organization. The author is the world's greatest satire writer so there may be factual errors in this book. All risk is on the reader.

ISBN

978-93-5437-713-6 (paperback)

Introduction

The first edition of this book was about investing in the Indian stockmarket but it remained popular around the world. This was because it:

- was, as the cover says, **a plain-English guide to investing in the stockmarket**. It assumed that you did not know anything about how stocks, company law, finance or commerce.
- had some useful 'extra' information that you will not find in any investment book and no business school will teach you. Mere textbook knowledge will not help you understand the markets. Markets are influenced by news and information (there is a difference). **You need to know how to interpret the news with historical context**. (This book also teaches you some history, making it all the more interesting.)

This is why one reader wrote:

> I recently came across your eBook "How to Invest In Stocks", and just wanted to let you know I think it is a very well written introduction to the markets!
>
> Although your book obviously in tune with your home market in India, it still works very well for any market around the world (I work in both UK and France). I wish I had come across your paper many years ago! It's a great read...

While this completely revised second edition retains the original premise, it also has a global focus, updated information and new chapters. (I was also able to include several financial humour poems that I had written for my 2020 jokebook.) Today, the once-obscure task of stock trading has become trivial, as it is entirely electronic. For most investors, it is only slightly different from many other things they buy online. Almost every bank today (in India) provides a trading account as part of their online service. Although this book does show how to buy/sell stocks online, **the stock-trading service provider you finally choose will have the best guide to their service**. This book has a broader perspective.

If you have any comments or suggestions, please mail them to Info@VSubhash.Com.

Contents

Introspection

Before you seek answers to your questions, try asking yourself the following questions:

- What kind of investor do you consider yourself to be?
- Do you want to make a quick buck or do you want to invest for the long term?
- How much time are you willing to devote for research?
- How much money do you plan to invest?
- Are you looking for obscene amounts in profits or a gradual appreciation of your portfolio?
- Do you have the stomach to take some losses or see the value of your portfolio sink should that ever happen?

If someone gives you investment advice without asking such questions, then you are asking the wrong person.

What kind of investor do you consider yourself to be?

In India, there are plenty of risk-free investment options that provide high returns - bank deposits, post office savings, public provident fund, etc. An investor with limited financial knowledge can invest in any of them with his eyes closed. No worries, as nothing will ever go bad. If you want that level of comfort, then the stockmarket is not for you.

Do you want to make a quick buck or do you want to invest for the long term?

To make quick profits, you need a lot of experience. You need to devote a lot more time on research so that you do not lose your shirt on bad investments. Only very sharp operators know when to quickly move in and out. This book is not for such investors as it is not something a book can teach.

Even if you are new to the markets, you can still make small investments every month and grow your portfolio. Such a diversified portfolio will serve your retirement needs well, even if some investments go bad.

How much time are you willing to

devote for your research?

If you are like me when I began investing, i.e., investing on the side while having a regular day job, then this book is for you. In the morning, I would read the daily newspaper and go to work. On the way, near the railway station, I would buy a copy of *The Economic Times* and read it on the train. In the evening, I would watch *CNBC*, apart from ordinary TV news channels. During the weekends, I would read *BusinessWorld* magazine. To be an investor in the market, you need to devote time for research. If you cannot do the research but stay in the market, then you will be like driving a car in the fog — you will crash eventually.

How much money do you plan to invest in stocks?

I am not a financial advisor (who works on a commission basis) so I will not advise you to invest everything you have in stocks. Stocks is one of several investment opportunities. Invest only a portion of your funds in stocks.

Investment	Amount
Bank deposits	20%
Stocks & bonds	20%
Real estate	20%
Gold	20%
Cash	20%

Are you looking for obscene amounts in profits or a gradual appreciation of your portfolio?

Although I seen the former in several of my investments, it should never be your goal. A gradual rise in the value of your stocks over time is what you should expect. Despite the facade of sophistication, markets do sometimes behave in bizarre counter-intuitive ways. (You will learn more of this later.) Any unforeseen rise in profits should be seen only as an added bonus.

Do you have the stomach to take some losses or see the value of your portfolio sink should that ever happen?

Share prices can go high and they can go low. You should not let your mood follow the stock. If you pick a good stock, its value will increase over time. Some lows in the interim should not alter your faith in its long-term prospects.

Summary

It might have taken you years to save your money but you can lose it all in a few minutes in the stockmarket. You should not act rashly. Nobody has a surefire legitimate way to make a fortune off the stockmarket. Success is dependent on hard work and luck. Some guys get lucky without doing any work. Some others work hard and have no luck. However, being dependent on hard work is a surer way of success. As *Bhagvad Gita* suggests, do not let your worries about the outcome come in the way of doing what needs to be done. Just do your duty.

Now, if you think you are game for the stockmarket, it is time learn some basics.

What is a share?

Stock

Just as the cattle heads owned by a farmer is considered as stock, the investment made by a businessman in his venture is also known as **stock**. In case of the latter, the **stock** is not limited to shop items that are available for sale.

When a business is entirely owned by a person, he owns all the stock. When a business owner invites some others to invest in his business, he is conceding a portion of the stock to others. His ownership is getting diluted and the new investors are gaining stock ownership.

In a business that has multiple investors, there is one investor or a group of investors that runs the venture. This person/group is supposed to have **managerial control,** as he/they handle its day-to-day management decisions. This class of investors is known as the **promoter** or **promoter group**. Their stock is known as the **promoter stock** or **promoter's stake**. The promoter group can run the business only if it has majority of the stock with them or the support of majority of the investors. The exact percentage of this majority may vary with country to country or state to state.

Shares

A business can be entirely owned and run by a person and not registered as a company. An example would be a self-employed electrician/mechanic or the owner of a shop in your locality. Such a business is known as a **sole proprietorship.** The concept of 'shares' does not arise here, even if there are multiple investors.

A business that is registered with the government as a 'company' has a different profile. A **company**, by definition, is an association of multiple persons formed for the purpose of running a business venture. These multiple persons are investors in the company. During the formation of the company, their stock (investment) has been divided into lots of units known as 'shares'. These **shares** are units of equal value representing a piece of ownership in a company.

Suppose the total investment in a company is ₹2 crores (₹2,00,00,000 or ₹20 million). This investment can be converted into a stock of 20 lakh (2 million) *shares* of ₹10 each.

Number of shares	**=**	**Total investment ÷ Face value of a share**
20,00,000	=	₹2,00,00,000 ÷ ₹10

$$\text{Face value of a share} = \text{Total investment} \div \text{Number of shares}$$

$$₹10 = ₹2,00,00,000 \div 20,00,000$$

$$\text{Total investment} = \text{Number of shares} \times \text{Face value of a share}$$

$$₹2,00,00,000 = 20,00,000 \times ₹10$$

If the investment of the original owner or promoter is ₹1.2 crore (₹1,20,00,000 or 12 million) and that of other/new investors is ₹0.8 crores (80,00,000 or 8 million), then the promoter is allotted 12 lakh (12,00,000 or 1.2 million) shares and other investors get 8 lakh (8,00,000 or 0.8 million) shares.

Because every one of those shares are of equal value, the name 'equity' is used synonymously with that of shares or investment. Thus, a person's **equity** refers to his investments in the venture or the quantum of shares he owns in the stock.

In the days of physical trading...

Until a few decades ago, a company had to issue a **share certificate** to every **share holder**. This *share certificate* would look somewhat like a fixed deposit certificate from a bank. It served as proof of the investment. It would have the name of the share holder, the number of shares held by him and the par value of each share.

A specimen share certificate filed by a game company.

This certificate would be printed in a thick security paper and it would have a watermark and seal. It would have a serial number and be signed by a top company official. In case of old certificates, previous owners would have signed on the back. Just like a fixed deposit certificate, a share certificate could be used as collateral or security for a loan.

When a company receives funds from new investors, the new funds would be added to the existing stock. The combined stock (representing the total funds invested in the company) would then be split into shares, each with a certain **face value** or *value at par*. In India, ₹10 is a popular choice. If you gave ₹9,000 to invest in the company mentioned in the previous section, the company would have given you a share certificate mentioning that you are the owner of *900 shares of ₹10 at par*.

If it was a publicly traded company (i.e., if its shares were listed on a stock exchange), the certificates also served as tradeable commodities at the stockmarket. Depending on the current market price for shares from that company, you (the current shareholder) could make a profit or a loss when you sold the certificate to a buyer (the next or future shareholder).

You did not have to go physically in search of a buyer. The stockmarket exists for that very purpose. The stockmarket or more precisely the **stock exchange** is a place for buyers and sellers to trade shares under certain rules. You just give your share certificate to your local **stock broker**. This man would have been listed in the phonebook or had an office in your part of the town. He was actually a sub-broker of a real broker - a member of the stock exchange. (The stock exchange was a real building were stock brokers would visit and conduct their trades. Ordinary shareholders did not visit it. It was only for members.) Your broker will take the certificate from you and ask you to sign a transfer form and the share certificate. He will then find another stock broker at the stock exchange who has an investor interested in acquiring shares in the same company. (That investor would have already paid that broker for purchasing the required shares from some shareholder like you.) When your broker gets paid by the buyer's broker, he hands over the share certificate and transfer form. Your broker then pays you after deducting his commission. The buyer's broker adds the details of the buyer and mails the transfer form and share certificate to the company's shares department. The company updates its records with the buyer as the new shareholder. The updated certificate is then mailed to buyer's address.

This is fine but how did you invest in the company and acquire the share certificate in the first place? When you buy or sell shares, the stockmarket acts as the **secondary market**. As the name suggests, there is a different market that comes before this. That one is known as the '**primary market**'. When a company issues new shares to the public, it enters the *primary market*. This is done through a process known as an **Initial Public Offering (IPO)**. In an IPO, the company engages a **merchant banker** or an **underwriter** to handle the

IPO. The merchant banker notifies brokers, post offices, banks, and other agents about the IPO and gives them blank application forms. When you hear about the IPO from an ad in the newspaper or TV, you contact your broker or go to your bank or post office or whoever is issuing the IPO application forms. You fill up the form with details about you and the form of money you are investing. You then give the completed application form and the money to the agent or mail it to the address mentioned in the IPO application form. When the merchant bankers receives your money, it asks the company to issue equivalent shares to you.

This is how it happened just a few decades ago. Today, it serves as a good way of explaining what a share is. Another way is to use an example.

An example

Suppose that I am a sole proprietor (a one-man operation) who owns tea plantations. After drying and curing the tea leaves, I process and pack them for export. Like most exporters, I pack and ship the tea to some NRI (non-resident Indian) in the US who sells it to the supermarket chains there. As he corners most of the profits, I am thinking of selling it in India with my own network - on that will compete with the likes of HLL (Unilever) and Tata Tea.

For this massive expansion of the business, I need more capital (money). I do not want to borrow money from banks because the the amount is huge and they will need collateral (assets that can be seized in case I am unable to repay).

Now, I am thinking of the stockmarket. By issuing shares in the market, I will get money to fund the business expansion. I do not have to pay any interest to my shareholders. I have to pay them only when I make a profit. If the venture fails, the loss is borne by shareholders. My loss, in that case, would be limited to the number of shares I own.

This is how businesses think when they issue shares. When a sole proprietor runs a business, he bears all the risk. He invests all the money and he takes all the profits. When a business issues shares, new investors are brought in and they ALL share the ownership, risks AND profits/losses in proportion to their holdings (share ownership).

Incorporation

A sole proprietorship cannot issues shares in the primary market. First, it needs to convert itself into a company. In India, this involves registering as a

limited-liability joint-stock company with a state government. This process is known as *incorporation*. In India, it will include the submission of a Memorandum of Association (MoA) and an Article of Association (AoA). These documents describe the purpose of the company, how it will be formed and function and what are the rights/obligations of shareholders and management.

As a **body corporate**, I may apply for a name such as *Subuntu Tea Company Private Limited.*

Subuntu Tea Co. Pvt. Ltd.	India
Subuntu Tea LLC	USA
Subuntu Tea PLC	UK
Subuntu Tea Gmbh	Germany

A *joint-stock company* is a commercial association of multiple individuals to run a business. A sole proprietor or owner will have to issue shares to somebody else, even if he retains majority ownership. This is not really a problem.

My tea company can convert my stock (investment of ₹2 crores or ₹2,00,00,000) into 20 lakh shares. It can issue 19,99,000 shares to me and 1000 shares to one or more relatives or friends whom I choose. I can even get it to allot all but one share to me and one share to another person.

India, like several other countries, now allows one one-person companies so that friendless people can also form companies. Statutory compliance can be a hassle so being a one-person company has its advantages.

There are many advantages of becoming a company. One of them, in my opinion, is that a body corporate is taxed only on profits, not on nett income. Besides that, a company can offset profits against past losses. It can also move profits into a reserves account. This reduces the declared profit while holding the bulk of the real profit in abeyance of a future expenditure.

When the company is registered with the government, an *article of association* is submitted. This will mention how many shares have to be issued to the shareholders. This is known as the **authorised capital** or the **capital base** of the company. When the shares are paid for, it is known as the **paid-up share capital.** When a share is listed in the stockmarket, the current price of the share multiplied by the number of shares represents its **market capitalisation.**

Preference Shares

The shares described so far are known as common stock. There is another class of shares known as **preference shares**. These are issued to investors who do not care about the profits that the company may or may not be making. They need a fixed return on their investment. The owners of preference shares are paid before dividends are paid for common stock holders. These shares usually do not have voting rights.

Convertible Debentures

Some companies issue debt with the option to convert them into common stock. Sometimes, when a distressed company is renegotiating its loans, it may suggest that its lenders convert the loans into convertible debentures. Like shares, debentures are not backed by any collateral.

There exists another debt instrument called **Non-Convertible Debentures (NCDs)**. An NCD is like a corporate bond or company deposit, and cannot be converted into stock.

Initial Public Offering (IPO)

One! Two! The money won't do!
Three! Four! The angels hit the road!
Five! Six! The IPO fails!
Seven! Eight! The promoters get out!
Nine! Ten! No one's laughin'

— From my book *2020 Fresh Clean Jokes For Everyone*. This poem is set to the tune of the nursery rhyme *One, two, buckle my shoe*.

After a few years of successfully running as a privately owned company, a private company can enter the **primary market**. Many tech companies do not even wait to make profits. They enter the primary market on the back of promises. This is usually done at the behest of venture capitalists who seek to offload their stock immediately after a successful IPO.

Because a company's main business is not dealing with shares and the stockmarket, they appoint some specialized companies called *merchant bankers* to do the job. The merchant bankers are the ones who approach the share market and manage the IPO on behalf of the company.

An important thing that the merchant banker will do is arrange for a 'crediting rating' by a **credit rating agency**. This agency will assess the risks associated with investing in the IPO and give a commensurate investment rating. A typical 'A' rated security is considered investment-grade. B-rated securities are considered to have certain risks associated with them.

The share application will be accompanied by an **offer document**, which will provide background information about the company, its promoters, reasons for the issue (of shares in the primary market), their business plan, risk factors, credit rating and other valuable information.

You, as an investor, will come to know about the IPO when the merchant banker issues advertisements in newspapers and other media. If you read a financial newspaper, you will learn about it much earlier.

If you have an online share-trading account, you will be able to download the offer document from the account's IPO section. If not, you will be able to access it from the website of the stock exchange, merchant banker or the offer-issuing company.

IPO   Buyback   Takeover

Name (Type)	Min. Qty	Price Band/ Floor Price (Rs.) (Max Retail Value)	Qty Multiples	Start/End Date & Time	Action
FIRST CALL ADITYA BIRLA FASHION AND RETAIL LTD : ADIPP1	1	27.50 - 27.50 Rs 2481618655.00	1	15-JAN-2021 10:00:00 29-JAN-2021 15:00	Go

The offer period lasts only a few days. It has an **opening date** and a **closing date** during which completed applications will have to be received by the merchant banker. In an online trading account, you will have to apply to purchase these shares. Sometimes, shares will only be available in lots of 100 or whatever number specified by the merchant banker. Because there are few IPOs at any given time, most of the lots are usually picked up on the first day itself.

After the IPO, shares will be allotted by the issuing company's **registrar**. This **registrar** may be a different outfit or the company's own shares department ('investor relations' division). If the merchant banker gets more applications than the share lots that are available, that is, when the issue is oversubscribed, then the registrar will not allot shares for some applicants and will ask the merchant banker to refund their money.

Some companies will try to accommodate all retail applicants (investors like you). This means the applicant will definitely get some shares allotted but not all of what he had applied for. The rest of the money will be refunded.

Stock listing

After the IPO and share allotment is over, the company's **scrip** (share) will be listed on the stock exchange. The company has officially entered the **secondary market**.

Note here that shares get to be known as scrip, stock, stake, equity, security and investment under different circumstances. Each name has a different nuance to it.

When *Reliance Industries Limited (RIL)* issued shares in the primary market, it shares may have listed at ₹10. As the company made profits year after year, the scrip's value on the stockmarket increased. If today, the RIL share is at

₹1900 (ignoring all the stock splits and bonus shares), then the guy who bought RIL shares at ₹10 stands in for a huge profit.

Now, don't you go to your share broker's office and say with a straight face that you want to buy RIL shares from the primary market at ₹10. You will be laughed off. RIL had left the primary market decades ago when its IPO was subscribed. So has every company listed in the secondary market.

Not every company that entered the primary market has had its price go up in the secondary market. A lot of companies disappear without a trace. Many others trade below the prices that they were subscribed. Some shares become illiquid i.e., not many people trade in them. Suppose that your unfortunate scrip is shown to have last traded at ₹7 and you want to get rid of it. If there is not much trading in the scrip, you will not find buyers for it even if you are ready to sell it at ₹6.

An astute investor will do his homework by reading the offer document, evaluating the company's past performance and the track record of the promoters, etc., before buying shares in the primary market.

Sometimes, when a company with enviable track record and goodwill wants to enter the primary market, their merchant banker will tell the promoters say, "Hey! You don't have to issue shares at par. Let's charge a premium." This is how *Bharthi Telecom* came to the market at ₹40 for shares worth ₹10, while the lesser−known *Allahabad Bank* issued shares at ₹10 on par.

So, is a company that charges a premium the obvious choice? The answer is 'not necessarily'. When the first edition was written, Bharthi Telecom was trading below its IPO issue price while Allahabad Bank was trading above par. Why? The rollout of WLL networks by Reliance Industries Limited put a question mark over other cellular operators like Bharthi. The low−interest rate regime of the Reserve Bank allowed a bank like Allahabad Bank to give out more loans and make more money. The Securitisation Bill then passed by the Parliament also helped, as it allowed banks to recover bad loans more easily. (By the time of this second edition, the Bharthi has become one of the biggest Indian telecom companies. However, it is also one of the most indebted companies. It share price has risen high because of its marquee investors and inclusion in FII indexes. Allahabad Bank, being a government bank, has slipped from one banana peel to another. Because the government bails it out, its share price has not totally crashed. The government is seeking to amalgamate it with another government bank.)

If an IPO fails to attract enough subscriptions, then the merchant banker or the underwriter will have to buy the shares themselves so that the company can list on the stock exchange without delay and early investors can exit at a profit. The Facebooks IPO was marked by 'glitches' on listing day and the share price tanked. Morgan Stanley and other underwriters helped themselves to a hundred million dollar worth of Facebook shares without having to go through the IPO like an ordinary investor.

Trading & settlement

A stock exchange is formed by its brokers. Membership is limited. Most brokers in the real world are sub-brokers of the members of the stock exchange. There are brokers who specialize in companies in a particular sector, such as Information Technology (IT) or Fast-Moving Consumer Goods (FMCG). Some others deal with all kinds of stocks.

Indian stock exchanges like the BSE and NSE open at 9 a.m. and close at 3.30 p.m. The first 15 minutes form a pre-opening session during which orders can be placed but not be cancelled. On a typical day, lakhs of shares go through a broker's desk. A share's price may change every second depending on the interest in the scrip and the volume of the trades.

A broker may sell shares of a company in the morning and then buy it in the evening. He may do it vice versa. He may try both several times a day. It depends on the orders he is getting from his clients. There are several ways in which he can make money from transactions made over the course of one day:

- With each trade (buy or sell), he takes a percentage as commission.
- He can buy lots of shares in one scrip in the morning and then sell all of them later in the day when the price rises, even marginally. For example, *Indian Oil Corporation (IOC)* opened today at 100.30 and ended at 103.00. If the broker had bought, 10 lakh shares in the morning and liquidated them in the evening before close, he would have made ₹2,70,000 (10,00,000 × ₹2.70).
- He can accept an order to sell shares at some price, sell at a higher price, pay the customer at the contracted price, and pocket the change.
- He can accept an order to buy shares at some price, buy at a lower price, pay the customer at the contracted price, and pocket the change.

Because brokers tend to speculate with clients' money or borrowed money, there have been spectacular shocking market crashes. As always, the hardest hit in such crashes were retail investors (ordinary blokes like you and me). Because we do not sit in front of trading terminals, we cannot take evasive action to limit our losses. To protect investors like us and to limit the risk to other stocks and the broader economy, the Indian market regulator **Securities Exchange Board of India (SEBI)** and the stock exchanges have built in several safety mechanisms.

Among them are circuit breakers, which force a halt in trading if the price fluctuates beyond a certain percentage. Another one is rolling settlement, which prevents brokers from cornering shares in the market without having to actually pay for them. If a broker's buys are more than his sells, the broker has to acquire the shares in to his trading account by paying cash. Or, if his sells are more than his buys, he has to deliver the shares (transfer them out of his trading account). There is no carryover beyond the settlement cycle.

For most of the transactions in the market, no shares actually change hands. In India, 98% of market transactions in any day are no-delivery speculative transactions. The brokers who buy them during the day, sell most of them before close unless they have a client who needs them in their account. This is informally called day-trading. The high volume of transactions makes these shares very liquid. When you or I go to the market to sell these share, the trades in those shares are executed immediately.

Rare IPO alternatives: Direct listing and SPACs

Some stock exchanges allow companies to bypass the IPO process and directly list their shares. When a company is well known and its listing is eagerly anticipated by investing public, it may not issue new shares or engage an underwriter. It will directly sell existing shares of exiting private investors to the public. The Swedish music streaming company Spotify directly listed on the NYSE in 2018.

A Special-Purpose Acquisition Company (SPAC) may be formed for the sole purpose of acquiring a privately held company, which may not be known at the time of formation. The SPAC will be liquidated and the funds returned if it does not make its acquisition in a time-bound manner.

I would advise new investors to steer clear of these two.

Summary

The investment made in a company is known as the stock, not just the goods it has for selling. Shares are apportioned ownership of investors in a company. In an IPO, the existed owners' stock is diluted/liquidated when shares are issued to new investors. Those with majority shares or majority support get to manage the company. The stock exchange provides a mechanism where new shares can be issued to the public and old shares can be bought and sold.

This section gave you the basics of shares and the stockmarket. The real world of stock trading not so simple. Before going to the real world, you need to how a company is managed and the relationship it has with its shareholders.

The Company & Its Members

When an investor buys a share of a company, he becomes part of the company i.e., a member. The shareholder becomes a partner in business as he has put money from his pocket into the venture. This is true even if he has bought only one share worth ₹10.

In a privately held company (whose shares are not publicly traded), all shares are with the promoter group. There is not much question about their management. In my tea company, I own all the shares. After achieving statutory compliance (paperwork done, accounts audited and taxes filed), I rule.

In a publicly traded company, the promoter group forms the management. However, there are strict disclosure and probity norms to support the interests of all shareholders. An individual shareholder can, if he wants to, inspect the company's account books. If he has any doubts or needs any clarification about the way that the company conducts its business, the company is duty bound to answer him.

This right is vested in him by the **Company Law**. If the shareholder feels for any reason that the company is misusing the funds or does not respond to his queries satisfactorily, he can file a complaint with the **Department of Company Affairs (DCA)** under the **Ministry of Finance**. DCA will then look into it in a time−bound manner and order the company to do the needful. (This might be a good time to remind you that you are living in India and you should not get any crazy ideas into your head.)

All companies are formed under the Company Law and conduct their business under its rules. For an ordinary shareholder, the go-to person in the company is the **Company Secretary** of the firm. He

- handles the documents and procedures with regard to the registration of the company with the DCA
- handles the IPO and issue of share certificates, dividends, etc.
- makes and attests statutory declarations for commencement of business, audited accounts etc.
- maintains the correspondence between the company and its shareholders and also between the DCA
- conducts and records board meetings

The company's business is headed by a managing director or a chairman or a designation to that effect. He is overseen by a **board of directors**. If there is a chairman, then he is the *chairman of the board*. The biggest shareholders of a company appoint their representatives to the board. The number of directors a promoter group can appoint is determined by the size of their shareholding. The directors of the board vote on crucial issues affecting the company. The voting is democratic.

In India, all publicly traded companies need to have independent directors on the board. These directors are appointed by the management but are expected to safeguard the interests of the shareholders in general, not that of the promoter group alone.

AGM

As per Company Law, every company must conduct an **annual general meeting (AGM)**. Invitations are sent to all shareholders ahead of the meeting. Shareholders are given a synopsis of the past year's performance, an outline of future plans, state of current business environment, etc. The past year's accounts are presented. A dividend in case of a profit is suggested. Future plans are also suggested. The management, in consultation with the promoter group, places several resolutions on the agenda of the meeting. All shareholders are expected to vote on these resolutions.

An ordinary investor's vote usually does not count much as his shareholding as a percentage of the total is very small. This is because the promoter family owns a big chunk of the shares. Financial institutions (FIs), such as insurance companies and pension funds, may hold another big slice of the shares. The directors of the promoter family/group votes for all the resolutions placed by the management. The FIs tips the balance. They usually make or break a resolution. Even though retail investors' vote do not have a serious impact, you can still go to the AGM and raise questions in public to the top officials of the company in an attempt to influence the voting.

Other corporate actions of interest

The most awaited information at an AGM is the amount of profit that was generated in the previous year and how much dividend is to be declared for shareholders. The **dividend** is the apportioned profit from the previous year, specified as a percentage of the par value of the share, that is distributed to shareholders. If a company declares 30% dividend, then every 10-rupee share will get 3 rupees. The dividend used to arrive as an A/C payee cheque in the mail but now the company directly credits the amount to your bank account.

Instead of offering all profits as dividends, a company may convert some of it as new shares. These shares will be given free of cost to existing shareholders based on their existing holdings. This is known as a **bonus issue** and the new shares are known as **bonus shares**. It expands the share capital (total shares or capital base) of the company.

The opposite of a bonus issue is a **buyback**. Here, the company uses some of its profits to buy shares from the shareholders at a premium to the current market price. The bought shares are extinguished from the capital base of the company.

After a share price has increased a lot, it becomes unaffordable to many small investors. (MRF is an example. It is set to cross ₹1 lakh in a few years.) A high price can even affect liquidity (ease of selling). In such cases, a company might effect a stock split. This does not result in an increase in the capital base of the company but the number of shares will increase as per the split ratio. For example, in a two-for-one stock split ratio, a shareholder with 50 shares will then have 100 shares. The face value of the share will be adjusted. The market will also factor in the stock split. For example, if the share were at ₹30 before the stock split, it will be quoting at ₹15 post-split.

When a company may also decide on a **rights issue** where it seeks fresh investments from existing shareholders (say, to retire debt or for some new expansion). The company may sweeten the deal by offering them at a discount to the current market price.

The bonus and split ratios may be ambiguously defined. Sometimes they include existing shares and other times they do not. A 2:1 bonus issue could be one new share for existing share making it two shares finally or it could be two shares for every existing share making it three shares finally. Check the wording in the press release or write to investor relationship department to make it clear.

Because shares change hands so often, the company might declare a **book closure** period when there is no trading or is limited (no deliveries). The last set of shareholders before book closure become eligible for dividends, bonus shares and share splits. The company may also declare a **record date**. If you are on the company's books as a shareholder on that date, you are eligible for the benefits. When a company's share enters the no-delivery period or goes past the *record date* (**ex-dividend**), the new buyers do not get the benefit declared by the company (until next time).

Sometimes, the board may approve a stock split when the share price has reached a high price. Every existing share gets a free extra share. The par value of the new shares will be reduced as per the split ratio.

Bankruptcy

When a company is unable to pay its creditors, it is declared insolvent. This may be voluntary or involuntary. Its remaining assets are then sold/auctioned by the creditors as per a court-ordered dissolution or liquidation. In some countries, a company can seek temporary protection from creditors and attempt to reorganize and get back into solvency. In the US, it is referred to as seeking 'Chapter 11' protection.

In an insolvency process, creditors have a pecking order. Those who have lent money against collateral are the first. They usually ask the court to let them seize these assets. Employees who are owed wages may be next. Contractors and suppliers may come after them. Bond holders and shareholders are always last and they usually get nothing.

If the company manages to come out of insolvency, it may issue fresh stock to new shareholder. It will cancel existing common stock shares as the original investment has been frittered away and new investors are not obligated to finance old stock holders.

Summary

A company is an association of individuals in a business venture. A shareholder who bought his shares from the stockmarket is considered a member of the company, even if he is not part of the management or the promoter group. The Company Law vests with the shareholder several rights and with the management several obligations.

Stock Exchanges

The sharemarket is one of the many markets in operation in India. The biggest of them all is the **money market**, which is much bigger than the stockmarket. This market mainly deals with government-backed securities (*debt instruments*). Because money market securities (G-Sec) are issued by the government (for deficit spending), it is considered risk-free. Banks and large financial institutions are the main players here because they have to mandatorily park a portion of their funds in G-Secs. (This is to avert a total wipeout.) The Reserve Bank of India (RBI) is a direct participant and is also the regulator of the market.

The Indian Parliament has enacted a law and created an agency to regulate the stockmarket. It is called the **Securities and Exchange Board of India (SEBI)**. Its American counterpart is known as **Securities Exchange Commission (SEC)**. The mandate of the SEBI is to oversee the operation of the different stock exchanges and protect the interests of the investor. It does not own the stock exchanges but functions like its police.

Indian/international stock exchanges

There are several stock exchanges in India. **Bombay Stock Exchange (BSE)** is one of the oldest in the world. It is also the biggest in India. Companies from all over India have listed their shares on the BSE. It used to operate like a fishmarket but now has a fully electronic trading system. In the US, you can compare it to the **New York Stock Exchange (NYSE)**. The newer **National Stock Exchange (NSE)** is BSE's closest competitor. It began with an electronic trading system from Day 1. It is like the American **Nasdaq** (National Association of Dealers Automated Quotes). A brick-and-mortar operation like McDonald's might list on the NYSE but a tech outfit like Microsoft will likely be found on the Nasdaq. Online share trading platforms (websites) in India deal with the BSE and/or NSE.

In most stock exchanges, traders sit in front of their computer screens and take orders from their customers on their phones. They enter their orders into their trading terminals and when the order is matched in the electronic trading system by some other broker, the trade is executed. Large financial institutions have computer programs that execute the trades just like a human broker. For example, when you login to your trading account and buy/sell some shares, the order is sent to the exchange by a software program running on the trading site's server computer. At the exchange, the computer program running the electronic trading system receives the order from the trading sites's server. If there is a matching buyer/seller for your price, the trading system executes the trade. If not, it will wait until a matching order is received and wil then execute it. In either case, no human intermediaries are involved.

For actively traded shares, the share prices change by the second. The stock exchange provides these changes in raw form to those who need them. Financial data service outfits like Reuters and Bloomberg supply this information to trading terminals of brokers and also (as wire services) to the wider world through newspapers and TV channels. Business news channels such as CNBC or Bloomberg display share prices in a scrolling ticker at the bottom of the screen. Many websites also provide the same information.

Indexes

Among the shares listed on the BSE, the most important among them is a list of top 30 shares. A derivative number formed from the price of these shares is called **BSE Sensitive Index** or **Sensex**. It is considered as a barometer of the nation's financial health. Since these top 30 shares represent a huge chunk of the total **market capitalisation** (total value of the shares at current price), their performance is chosen as a marker for the whole stock exchange.

Every stockmarket in the world has such indices. The NSE has its *Nifty*. The US for example has the DJIA (Dow Jones Industrial Average) and the S&P 500. The UK has the FTSE 100 (Footsie or Financial Times Stock Exchange 100). It is published by the namesake pink newspaper. Japan's *Nihon Keizai Shimbun* newspaper has the Nikkei 225 index. Apart from such benchmark indices, there are separate sector-wise indices. Telecom may have one. Oil and gas may have one.

In addition to shares, the movement of the indices in a stockmarket are also tracked very diligently. When there is a lot of selling, the index goes down. When there is a lot of buying, the index goes up. The direction of the index essentially reflects the mood of the market.

Lists

The shares listed on the BSE is spread over several lists. Financial newspapers like *Business Line* (from *The Hindu*) or *Financial Express* (from *The Indian Express*) several pages worth of share price information of the previous day's trade in these lists. This may include opening price, closing price, volume, day's high, day's low, one-year high and one-year low. They may also mention the **earnings per share (EPS)** and the consequent **P/E ratio** (current price divided by earnings per share) The BSE's group A and B lists are usually published. They represent the most traded shares in the market. Newspapers are the best medium for stock price information. In one look, you may be able to see data of hundreds of companies. Radio or TV cannot do it. Even websites do not provide so much information in a few pages.

One very important number that can be determined from the stock price is the P/E ratio. This is an indicator of how much the market has factored in the profits made by the company. A company with a high P/E ratio already is an expensive stock, as it already has a premium associated with it. A company with a low P/E ratio is undervalued and has scope for price rise or positive reevaluation. When you want good appreciation of the share price, it is better to pick a share with low P/E ratio and wait.

Corporate actions

The management of listed companies are expected to inform the stock exchange about important events, activities and meetings in the company. They will file important documents such as audited accounts and quarterly reports. The exchange will make this information available to investors and traders. The most interesting kind of information is related to dividends, bonus shares and shares splits. These are usually decided in quarterly, half-yearly and annual general meetings of a company. In these meetings, the management presents latest audited accounts. The board may also decide on interim/final dividends, bonus shares or share splits. Some companies broadcast their meetings. Others publish minutes of the meeting afterwards. After the meeting, they may also have a conference call with stock analysts and even a live Q&A with retail investors.

MoneyControl.com is run by the Indian partner of the CNBC channel. I visit it every day in the morning for financial news and for its regularly updated 'Corporate Actions' section.

Dividends Declared - View Dividends declared by companies during the year.

Board Meetings	AGM / EGMs	Bonus	Splits	Rights	Dividend	Book Closures

COMPANY NAME	DIVIDEND		DATE		
	Type	%	Announcement	Record	Ex-Dividend
Majesco	Interim	19480.00	11-12-2020	25-12-2020	23-12-2020
Rajesh Exports	Final	100.00	30-06-2020	-	23-12-2020
Anant Raj	Final	4.00	03-09-2020	-	22-12-2020
Bambino Agro	Final	16.00	13-11-2020	-	22-12-2020
Guj Mineral	Final	100.00	23-06-2020	-	22-12-2020
Inani Marbles	Final	2.00	30-06-2020	-	22-12-2020
Orient Beverage	Final	5.00	26-08-2020	-	22-12-2020

Corporate results

The stock exchange is the #1 source for information about listed companies. While audited financial results may require a chartered accountant to make sense out of them, there is usually extremely important information buried in the numerous explanations and caveats that auditors are forced to mention. This is because the accounts are sometimes given the Hollywood treatment and dressed up to hide gaping holes in the financing. Time for a joke from my jokebook.

> **Truth in numbers**
> **Numbers**: Numbers don't lie.
> **Statistics**: But, we do.

Business News

There are TV channels devoted to the stockmarket. CNBC and Bloomberg are well known examples. Financial newspapers provide a more comprehensive of individual companies than TV channels. Visiting their websites is not enough because a lot of their news is hidden under a paywall or tabs.

Among American websites, I used to visit Yahoo! Finance every day. It is now loaded with ads. I now visit Zerohedge.com and Marketwatch.com every day.

The *Keiser Report* on RT by Max Keiser and Stacy Herbert is good show for investors. However, Max is a big promoter of 'cryptocurrencies'. If you can ignore that, the rest of show is very informative and entertaining.

RT America has surprisingly good coverage of Western financial news. RT's guests speak freely. Unlike CNN, MSNBC or Fox, they do not censor their guests or blame it on a technical glitch.

Summary

A stock exchange provides a well-governed mechanism for trading in shares. Shares are traded by retail and institutional investors through brokers, who are members of the stock exchange. The share price movements and stock-related information are broadcast to the world and published on the Internet, TV, radio and newspapers.

Financial terms in stock analysis

To pick a stock, you may need to do in-depth study about the company's:

- **Immediate business environment**: If you are studying the Tesla stock, you need to study the automobile segment in general. Because Tesla is an electric vehicle (EV) maker, you may need to do research on battery technology and government policy on renewable energy as well.

- **Management**: A company is run by people. Who are they? What are their antecedents? What is their level of involvement in the management?

- **Financial statements**: A company's *balance sheet*, *profit & loss statement* and *cash flow statement* found in the audited/unaudited results published on the stock exchange's website will tell you all you need to know.

  Some knowledge in *financial accounting* will be helpful here. Books on this subject can be very big but you only need an introduction to double-entry accounting and then these three types of financial statements. Just go through the first few pages of this free book from: https://lyryx.com/introduction-financial-accounting/. You do not have to understand every line or paragraph.

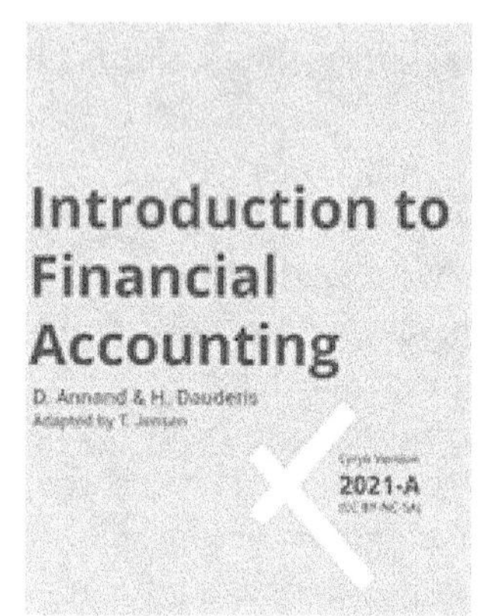

TV channels, newspapers and websites also provide detailed stock analyses so that you do not have to pore over raw numbers. It does not matter how or where you get your data, it is inevitable that you will encounter several new financial terms. It is important that you know what they are.

- **Memorandum of Association (MoA)**: This is the primary document that serves as the constitution of the company. It will specify the
  - name of the company
  - address of its registered office
  - nature and scope of operations
  - liability of members
  - authorised share capital

- **Articles of Association (AoA)**: This is secondary to the MoA of the company. It specifies the rules that will be followed in the management of the company. Among several things it specifies are the different classes of shares, how shares will be issued/forfeited, how profits (dividends) will be distributed, formation of board of directors, how meetings will be conducted and decisions passed, arbitration provisions and winding-up procedure.

- **Authorised share capital**: This is the value and number of shares that the company is authorised in the MoA for issuance to shareholders.
- **Common Shares**: These are the usual class of shares issued by companies. They provide a voting right to participate in the management, a share in the profits and a right to liquidated assets (in case of winding-up).
- **Preferrence Shares**: These are a special class of shares issued certain investors who will not have any voting power but will be paid a set dividend before owners of common shares.
- **Outstanding Shares**: These are the shares that have been issued and are held by shareholders.

Outstanding shares	=	Authorised shares *less* (—) Unissued shares *less* (—) Issued shares held by company (buyback, cancellation,…)

- **Assets**: These are valuable resources that are owned by a business. It can include cash, stock-in-trade, equipment, supplies and insurance. They represent the owners' original investment and reinvested profits.
- **Liabilities**: These are payments that have to be made in future. It can include loans, rent due, goods taken on credit, and payments taken in advance of delivery or performance.
- **Net Assets**: This represents the excess of assets over liabilities. It is what the business owners can call as their equity or networth.

Equity	=	Assets — Liabilities
Assets	=	Equity + Liabiliies

The first equation implies that the assets of a business is represented by the owners' equity and borrowings.

- **Fixed costs**: These are costs such as rent or employee salaries that have to be paid whether or not the business is in production or service.
- **Variable costs**: These are costs such as supplies or transportation that change with the volume of production.
- **Depreciation**: This is the loss of value of a tangible asset (something you can kick) over time. A brand-new desktop computer does not have the same value as one that is a year old. In fact, depreciation starts as soon as the asset is acquired or comes out of the packaging. Hence, it has to be deducted from the calculation of the assets owned by the

company. The depreciation rate is notionally based on the resale value and is usually specified by government for different classes of assets. The depreciation costs can be deducted from net profits and can lower taxes to be paid.

- **Amortisation**: This is the loss of value of an intangible asset (something you cannot kick) over time. An asset such as public goodwill or a licence/permit may have a cost of acquisition and a fixed life. This asset's value cannot be extinguished suddenly at the end of its usefulness. It has to be *written off* or *expensed* from the total assets at a predetermined rate over its life.

- **Net income**: This is the excess of revenue over expenses. If revenue is higher, then net income is positive or a net profit. If expenses are higher, then net income is negative or a net loss.

- **Gross profit**: This is excess of revenue from sales over cost of production. It is arrived at before deducting expenses such as taxes or interest.

- **Net operating profit**: This is the profit after deducting interest costs and taxes. It is also known as *operating income* or *earnings before interest and taxes* (**EBIT**).

- **Book value per share**: This is a measure of the actual net asset value available to the holder of a company's common stock. It is arrived by dividing the common equity by the number of outstanding shares. Stock buybacks reduce the number of outstanding shares and cause an increase in the book value. If the market price for a share is less than the book value, then the company is undervalued and may present an opportunity for *value investors*. Such shares usually see a sharp appreciation in market price in the wake of positive news.

| **Book value per share** | = | (Total Equity — Preferred Equity) ÷ Number of outstanding shares |
| **Book value per share** | = | (Assets — liabilities — liquidation price of preferred shares) ÷ Number of outstanding shares |

- **Earnings per share (EPS)**: This is the net income divided up by the number of outstanding shares.

| **EPS** | = | Net income ÷ Number of outstanding shares |

The net income is arrived after deducting the dividend paid to holders of preference shares. The outstanding shares refers to common shares and does not include preference shares. EPS provides the amount of income available for one common share. A high EPS is indicative of good performance by the company.

- **Price-to-Earnings (PE) ratio**: This ratio compares the current market price to the earnings per share (EPS).

PE ratio	=	Current market price of share ÷ Earnings per share

Overvalued shares have a high PE ratio. The upside in their share price may be limited. Undervalued shares have a low PE ratio. There may be considerable upside for their share prices.

- **Return on Capital Employed (RoCE)**: This ratio compares the net operating profit to the net assets of a company.

RoCE	=	(EBIT ÷ Net Assets) × 100
RoCE	=	((Profit — Interest — Tax) ÷ (Assets — Liabilties)) × 100

Capital employed is the net assets (owners' equity). RoCE is the proportion of operating profits in terms of the owners' equity or investment (net assets).

- **Debt-to-Equity ratio**: This ratio compares a company's debt to its owners' equity. It shows how *leveraged* the company's balance sheet is.

Debt-to-Equity	=	Total debt ÷ Owners' equity

Because lenders have to be paid before shareholders, this ratio shows how much debt hangs over the shareholders' investment. Companies with low debt-to-equity ratios are better off than others. However, companies with good prospects may have a high debt-to-equity ratio initially or when they are expanding. As they make profits, the debt load reduces and the ratio gets lowered.

- **Return-on-Equity (RoE)**: This ratio compares a company's net income to the owners' equity.

Return-on-Equity	=	Net income ÷ Owners' equity

- **Return-on-Assets (RoA)**: This ratio compares the profits to the assets of a company. It is simple way of determining how efficiently a company is generating profits.

Return-on-Assets	=	(Net income ÷ Assets) × 100

While RoE shows how well the owners investment has been used, RoA shows how well the owners' investment and borrowings have been used.

- **Earnings Before Interest, Tax, Depreciation & Amortisation (EBITDA):** This is the earnings of a company without deducting the costs of interest, tax, depreciation and amortisation.
- **Profit margin:** This is the percentage of the net profit to the revenue generated by the company.

Net profit margin	=	(Net profit ÷ Revenue) × 100
Operating profit margin	=	(Operating profit ÷ Revenue) × 100
Gross profit margin	=	(Gross profit ÷ Revenue) × 100

- **Asset turnover:** This ratio compares the total sales to the average assets of the company. It is a measure of how efficiently the company is using its assets to generate sales.

Asset turnover	=	Total sales ÷ Average assets
Asset turnover	=	Sales this year ÷ ((Assets at the beginning of year + Assets at the end of the year) ÷ 2)

- **Equity multiplier:** This ratio measures how much of a company's total assets are financed by owners' equity rather than by debt.

Equity multiplier	=	Total assets ÷ Owners' equity

- **Pledged shares:** These are shares that have been pledged by the owners as collateral for loans to the business. The owners will continue to be able to exercise their voting power but will not be able to sell them. Pledged shares are an indication of stressed nature of a business under extreme levels of debt.
- **Capital Adequacy Ratio (CAR):** This ratio compares a bank's core funds with its risk-weighted assets to measure how well it can absorb losses. As per Basel Liquidity Norms, the core funds are made up of by Tier 1 and Tier 2 capital. Tier 1 capital refers to funds that are required to absorb losses without having to temporarily cease functioning. Tier 2 capital refers to funds that are required to absorb losses in case the bank is forced to wind up. Tier 2 capital offers lesser protection to depositors and creditors. Tier 1 includes its share capital and audited reserves (retained profits) less (subtracted by) audited losses and investments in subsidiaries. Tier 2 refers to unaudited reserves and earnings. Tier 2 is

what remains after Tier 1 is depleted. The assets are calculated differently based on risk. For cash and investments in government securities (statutory reserves), the weightage is 0%, as there is no risk. For the personal loans, weightage may be 100%. A banks is expected to regularly reassess its loan portfolio and make adjustments to its capital tiers so that adequate CAR is maintained. The national banking regulator sets the CAR norm and tracks the CARs of banks under its purview.

- **Non-Performing Assets (NPAs)**: These are loans (in the books of a bank or other financial institution) that have gone bad or are unlikely to be repaid in full.
- **Current And Savings Account (CASA) ratio**: This ratio is used to measure a bank's cost of funds. It compares the funds deposited by the bank's customers in current/savings accounts with that of total deposits. Because banks pay no or less interest on these accounts, the cost of these funds is lower than that of fixed deposit accounts.
- **Credit Deposit (CD) ratio**: This ratio compares the funds lent by a bank to those deposited with it. **A bank lends at a higher interest rate than it pays for deposits.** This ratio examines how much of the funds deposited with it are being loaned out. A lower ratio indicates that the bank is not making optimum use of the funds deposited with it.
- **Net Interest Margin**: This is the difference between the profit a bank or a financial institution makes off loans and the interest it pays to depositors.
- **Capital Gains Tax**: This is the tax levied on profits from the sale of an asset. The asset can be anything from real estate to shares. The tax rate is dependent on the interval between the acquisition and the sale. Tax rates for long-term capital gains and short-term capital gains are usually different.
- **Dividend Tax**: This tax is levied in some countries on the dividend that is distributed to shareholders. The tax may be deducted at source by the company (TDS) or in the hands of the shareholder (when filing for income tax returns).
- **Transaction Tax**: This tax has been suggested for imposition on financial transactions. If imposed on day-trading or no-delivery transactions, it may bring down volumes to near zero, as the margins are usually wafer-thin. Transaction tax is usually imposed on for-delivery transactions. In India, it has been imposed on bank ATM transactions and account transfers too.
- **Tax deduction**: This is an income head that can be deducted from the gross income (entirely or by a fraction) when calculating the tax due.
- **Tax exemption**: This is an income head that need not be included in

the gross income when calculating the tax due.

- **Yield-to-maturity (YTM)**: This is the total (anticipated) interest earned from a fixed-rate bond over its lifetime — when it is held to its maturity date (not sold prematurely). It is usually highest when the debt instrument is bought (without a premium) at the time of issue. Fixed-rate bonds are usually priced above prevailing bank interest rates. Investors hold bonds to maturity to be shielded from risk associated with changes in interest rates or bond prices (both of which are inversely related). They 'lock in' the interest rates.

Your Demat Account & Online Trading

In the chapter *What is a share* [8], I mentioned that in the past IPO allottees were given printed share certificates. It is not so anymore. Whether you want to buy shares from the primary market or the secondary market, you need to have a share holding account called the *demat* account.

Demat is an abbreviation of dematerialisation. When share trading moved from physical to an online system (electronic trading system), the physical share certificates underwent a process known as dematerialisation. A dematerialised share exists only in computer databases (maintained at an institution known as a **share depository**).

A share trading services provider holds your shares at the depository as a **depository participant (DP)**. If you have a bank account with ICICI Bank, then they can provide you with a share trading account. In this case, they act as a DP. This DP holds your shares with the National Securities Depository Limited (NSDL) or the Central Depository Services Limited (CDSL), which acts as their depository. As an investor, you only need to interact with ICICI Bank (the DP) and not with NSDL/CDSL (the depository).

In Western countries, they have eliminated terms like demat. You just have a share trading or a brokerage account. Things like demat or depository is too much information. All trading is paperless. They do not know anything about paper.

Trading account

In India, most banks provide share trading services. You need to ask your bank manager or some other official to enable that facility. The bank will ask you fill out some KYC (Know Your Customer) forms and then your saving account will be linked to a new demat account and a share trading account. A username and password for your share trading account will then be mailed to you. After you login and change your password, the account will be ready for trading. Because the share trading account is linked to your bank account, allocating money for trading is just a click away. All dividends and sales proceeds will be credited to your bank account automatically. The whole process is seamless.

If you got your share trading account from some other provider, then you may have to transfer money out of your banking website and into the walled garden of your share trading provider. However, dividends and sales are proceeds are automatically credited to your bank account, just like in the previous case. (When you start a demat account, it is linked to your bank account.)

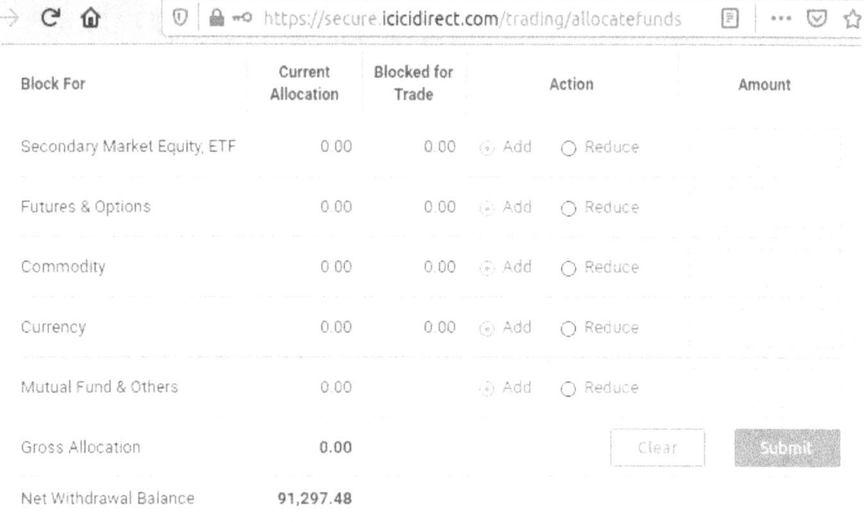

Buying/selling shares online

Every share or security listed on a stock exchange has a code associated with it. When buying shares, you can type the name of the stock or the stock code. The website will then correctly guess the stock or ask you to choose from a list. After the correct share is identified, the site will list the price at which the share is trading or last traded. You can then specify the quantity of shares you want to buy.

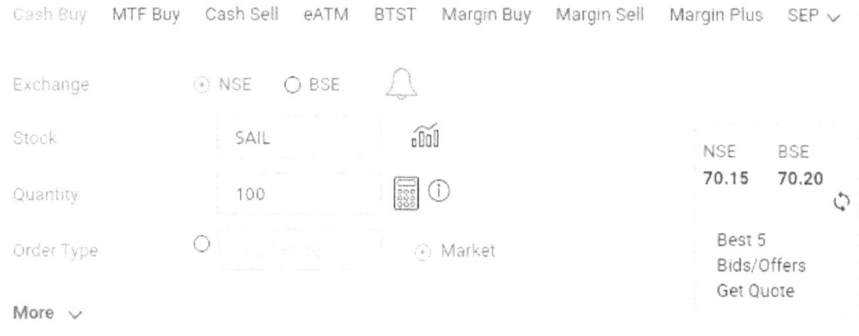

You can then specify the price at which want to buy the shares in one two ways:

- **Limit Order:** You specify a price at which you want to buy or sell the shares. If there are matching orders for that price at that time, then stock exchange will execute the order. That is, for a limit buy order, there should be offers at the specified price or below it. If you made a limit buy order for ₹12 and there were offers for ₹10 and ₹9 that day, your order will be executed at ₹9. For a limit sell order, there should be matching order at the price you specified or above it. If you made a limit sell order at price ₹20 and there were bids that day at ₹21 and ₹22, your order will be executed at ₹22.

Order Type	:	○ Market ◉ Limit
Limit Price	:	
Stop Loss Trigger Price	:	?

If there were no matching orders until trading close (closing time), your order will not be executed and marked as *expired*. When a share is rising and remains higher than the price you specified (for the rest of the day), your limit buy order will not get executed. Similarly, when a share if falling and remains below the price you specified (for the rest of the day), your limit sell order will not get executed.

When an order does not get executed, there is an opportunity loss. To avoid it, you can specify a range around the price you specify in your limit order in which the trade can still be executed. This is known as a stop-loss trigger price. For example, when you want to sell a share at ₹20, you can specify a trigger price of ₹18. Even if there was just one bid at ₹18.20, the trade will still be be executed. Similarly, when you want to buy a share at ₹72 but the share is available only at ₹80, you can specify a stop-loss trigger price of $76. Should the price ever come down to ₹76, ₹72 or even ₹70, your order gets executed.

- **Market Order:** You specify that the shares be bought or sold at whatever the current market price is. Share prices can change by the second. By the time, you check the price and place your market order, the current price could have changed quite a bit and your order may get executed at a different price.

Order Type	:	◉ Market ○ Limit
Limit Price	:	
Stop Loss Trigger Price	:	?

When a share is rising, a market buy order may get executed at a higher price than when you made the order. This increases the cost price for you. Suppose, you made a market order when the price was ₹60 and the order got executed only when an offer was available at ₹67, then your cost has increased by ₹7 per share.

To prevent a market buy order from snagging a very high price, you can specify a stop-loss trigger price. For example, you can specify a stop-loss trigger price of ₹62. Now, if the price remains above that price for the rest of the day, the trade will not be executed.

Similarly, when a share is falling, a market sell order may get executed at a lower price than when you made the order. This decreases the selling price for you. Suppose, you made a market sell order for ₹70 and the order got executed at ₹62, whatever profit you had expected would have been reduced by ₹8 per share.

To prevent a market sell order from getting executed at a too-low price, you can specify a stop-loss trigger price of ₹68. This means that the share will be sold at best at ₹70 and worst at ₹68.

Of course, when you specify a stop-loss trigger price, the trade may not get executed at all. The trade will be shown as *expired* at the end of the day. *A market order will be definitely executed if you do not specify a stop-loss trigger price.*

You can issue a market buy order without a stop-loss trigger price if you expect the share to rise in future, above any intra-day high over the rest of the day. You can issue a market sell order without a stop-loss trigger price if you are sure that the price may not recover at all in future or you need to exit it whatever the cost.

- **Stop Order**: This is something day traders or margin traders use. My investment philosophy is wholly against the concept so I will only briefly mention it here. This is a second order placed after a limit or market order. It is designed to do the opposite of the previous order in order to square their positions - restore their previous position when the share did not move in the direction they expected. A guy may buy some share expecting it to rise but will follow it up with a stop order to sell the same quantity if the share were to go down. Similarly, when he sells a share expecting it to fall, he may use a stop order to buy the share if it were to rise. The stop order remains in the system and gets executed only when the specified price is reached.

In my opinion, stop orders are not advisable because it is usually prudent to manually choose the time when a share is bought or sold. Suppose the 90-rupee share goes to ₹200 a few weeks after your stop order got executed... Or, after the 20-rupee share momentarily dipped below ₹17 because of some rumours that was later cleared up ... Do you want to be sitting there looking like an idiot?

Cancel orders

You can cancel orders that have not been executed yet. Go to you order book or whatever they call it in your trading system, select your order and cancel it.

Demat Balance

When you make a buy order and it gets executed, the new shares will be added to your demat account. When you make a sell order (of course you must previously own the said shares) and it gets executed, the shares will be deducted from your account. In India, trades are settled on the same day after closing. (Rolling settlement was instituted after the previous stock market crashes. Earlier, settlement could take a month.) When you buy shares, the amount will be deducted from your account immediately. When you sell shares, it may take a day or two after execution of the order. How do you like that?

Order validity

Usually, orders are valid for a day. You could however specify that it be valid for several days, weeks or even months. You may also be able to make orders **Valid Till Cancel (VTC)**. Alternatively, you can specify an **Immediate Or Cancel (IOC)** validity to ensure that your order is either executed at the current price or not at all.

Transaction security

Although there are mobile apps for share trading, I would not suggest you use them. Use their website in a desktop browser. Use a wired LAN connection whenever you are doing financial transactions. Wireless routers are easily hijacked by hackers and malware. Free wireless networks may connect you to rogue DNS servers. Companies like Google and Apple save your wireless network password to their servers. Who knows what jerk you offended works there? You can use a wired connection to a wireless router in your home but disable its wireless networks. The network switch, DHCP server and other services provide will continue to function.

Your mileage may vary

This book provides only generic advice. The trading setup and rules could be different from country to country, exchange or exchange or trading service provider to another. This book is no excuse for not being familiar with the rules and practices that are applicable in your specific case. Consult your share trading service provider and apprise yourself with correct details. The nomenclature used by them could be very different so exercise extreme care.

For example, a market order with the BSE is like a regular market order. But, with the NSE, it can be different. If a market order was not executed on the NSE for some reason, it will get changed to a limit order (with the limit price set to the last traded price) on the next trading day.

How will you know about that kind of details? By reading their rule books and FAQs (Frequently Asked Questions). Do not worry about the rule books. The language is usually dumbed down for ordinary investors.

Bonds and other investment options

Your trading service provider may allow you to buy and sell quite a variety of securities. I am a conservative investor. I invest only in shares and bonds. Other forms are too opaque or risky for me.

A lot of retail investors, particularly retirees, invest in mutual funds. A **mutual fund (MF)** is an investment scheme where a designated **asset management company (AMC)** invests in shares and other securities on your behalf. A mutual fund assumes that you are too busy or ignorant to pick the stocks yourself while they have dedicated stock analysts or investment team just for that purpose. Like a share, a mutual fund is sold with face value but each security is known as a MF unit. The MF units are listed on the stock exchange and you can buy and sell them just like a share. The AMC publishes a daily tally called **net asset value (NAV)** for their mutual fund schemes. NAV is the average value of investments per unit after deducting expenses or liabilities. I do not invest in MFs because I know how to invest in stocks and the MFs have a certain opacity to them. Some MFs have some marquee stock pickers but most are made by a group of unknowns. MF investors rarely check their details even though their profiles are listed on stock exchange. If you are have time to do the research and pick the best MF, why not spend that time on stock analysis and directly invest in shares?

Options are another form of investments that is not easy to wrap your mind on. If you have heard about *puts* or *calls* in the stockmarket reports, well those are *put options* or *call options*. They provide you with an option (not an obligation) to buy or sell a stock at a predetermined price in future. These securities can be bought from the fancily titled *futures market*. If you are new to investing, stay away from it.

Here is a funny poem I wrote on the subject for my book *2020 Fresh Clean Jokes For Everyone*. The poem is set to the tune of the nursery rhyme *Little Jack Horner*.

> An options trader
> Sat in a corner
> Looking at his puts and call

He was ready to jump out of the window
When he heard a knock on his door
It was a pension fund that will take the fall

Derivatives are the most opaque investment options. Its main attraction is the opacity. The opacity is used to hide the toxicity of the underlying securities. However, big trading firms and news media tries to sell them as a 'sophisticated financial instruments'. The 2008 financial crash was caused by toxic derivatives. Future payments from dubious debt (loans given to those with poor credit) were bundled into a form of a security!. The sellers promised to stand in case of defaults (loans turning bad). This promise was sold to investors as *credit default swaps* but when a lot of underlying securities turned toxic (bad loans) the sellers did not have the money to fulfill the promise. The US government had to bail them out. Place for another poem. This one is set to the tune of *Bits Of Paper*.

C-D-S!
C-D-S!
Toxic 'n' infectious!
Toxic 'n' infectious!
Makes the banks look unsteady!
Makes the banks look unsteady!
Bail them out!
Bail them out!

Most of the sellers were private financial institutions including foreign-owned ones. Because the failure to pay would have affected the credit rating of the US as a whole and have catastrophic consequences across the rest of the world, the US government wrote a giant cheque on the backs of future US citizens. The 2008 bailout was so huge that the US could have paved its highways with gold using that money.

							Set Default
ICICI Bank FD	ICICI HFC FD	Corporate FD	GOI issuances	Other	Capital Gain Bond	Corporate Bonds	NCD/Bond

Fixed Deposits	Rating	1 Yr	2 Yr	3 Yr	4 Yr	5 Yr	Sr. Citizen %	Action
ICICI Bank Limited New	MAAA	4.90	5.00	5.15	5.35	5.35	0.50	Go

Bonds are simple investments. They are like fixed deposits at a bank. The difference being that the issuer is a corporate (company or mutual fund) or sovereign (local, state or national government) entity. You can understand its terms easily. A **bond** is an investment that gets locked in for a pre-determined duration in the business of the issuer. At the end of this time, the bond is said to have **matured** and the issuer will refund your entire principal investment back to you. During the investment lock-in period, the issuer will pay interest to you at regular intervals or as a whole at maturity. The only homework you need to do is to check whether the seller has a solid business and the interest rate is competitive when compared to those offered by your bank.

Bond types include company deposits (CDs), corporate bonds, non-convertible debentures (NCDs) and sovereign (government) bonds. With the exception of sovereign bonds, bonds are not backed by any collateral and are issued in good faith that the issuer will pay. The interest rate offered by these debt instruments may be known as their **coupon rate**. The interest is directly credited to the bank account that is linked to your trading account.

Apply For   POWER FINANCE CORPORATION LTD - JAN21 : PFCN28

ASBA ☑

Opt	Face Value	Interest Payout Frequency	Tenure	Coupon rate % per annum	Effective Yield % per annum	Demat Flag	Buyback Flag	Qty	Amount
I	1,000.00	Annual	3 years	4.80%	4.80%	☑	☐		
II	1,000.00	Annual	5 years	5.80%	5.80%	☑	☐		
III	1,000.00	Quarterly	10 years	6.82%	6.99%	☑	☐		
IV	1,000.00	Annual	10 years	7.00%	7.00%	☑	☐		
V	1,000.00	Annual	10 years	Benchmark FIMMDA 10Yr G-Sec (Annualised)+ 80 BPS	-	☑	☐		
VI	1,000.00	Quarterly	15 years	6.97%	7.15%	☑	☐		
VII	1,000.00	Annual	15 years	7.15%	7.15%	☑	☐		

Compare Scheme Details   Total

Payment Source   ⦿ Allocation

Relationship Code   Submit   Clear

In the US, **junk bonds** are also known as high-yield bonds. A junk bond has to offer higher interest because they are riskier and have received a non-A credit rating.

Summary

The stockmarket offers a lot of investment options. I suggest you study the markets for a year before actually investing anything. Some sites allow you to 'game' the stockmarket - you buy and sell virtual copies of actual shares at actual prices without spending any real money. This will allow you to critically examine your investment instincts without facing any real risk.

Stock Research and Portfolio Management

Buying when stocks are rising and selling when they are falling is utter stupidity. Never follow the herd. Do your own research. Have your own strategy. Make your own picks. Do not let the headless chickens that run around in a frenzy ever influence you.

Where to begin

You have read this book and you are ready to invest. What should you choose? **Do not!**

First, become familiar with the market. Read a financial newspaper from the first to the last page. Watch the business news channel. Do the news reports connect? What you have read/seen before and what you are reading/seeing now should have some relation. Over time, you should be able to connect what is happening in economy and what is happening the market. If it does not, then you are still new to the market. Give it a year of just following the news. Focus on a few market segments. Invest in a few stocks that you know for sure will do well in future.

Tracking stocks

Most stock trading sites and several financial news sites allow you to maintain an online portfolio for stocks.

Once you add a stock, they automatically show you the latest news reports mentioning those stocks.

You can also use RSS to track stocks. RSS is a popular technology used by websites to publicise their latest content. The sites publish links to the latest articles in a special link or URL that is known as the 'RSS feed'. You use this RSS feed link in an 'RSS reader' or 'news reader' software. RSS reader functionality are usually integrated into Internet browsers and email clients (Seamonkey). If not, they may be available using add-ons or extensions. RSS readers are also available as dedicated standalone apps (RSS Owl, LifeRea). RSS readers make it easy to read articles or article snippets from multiple news source in one place. The RSS feed may have the entire article or just a snippet of the linked article.

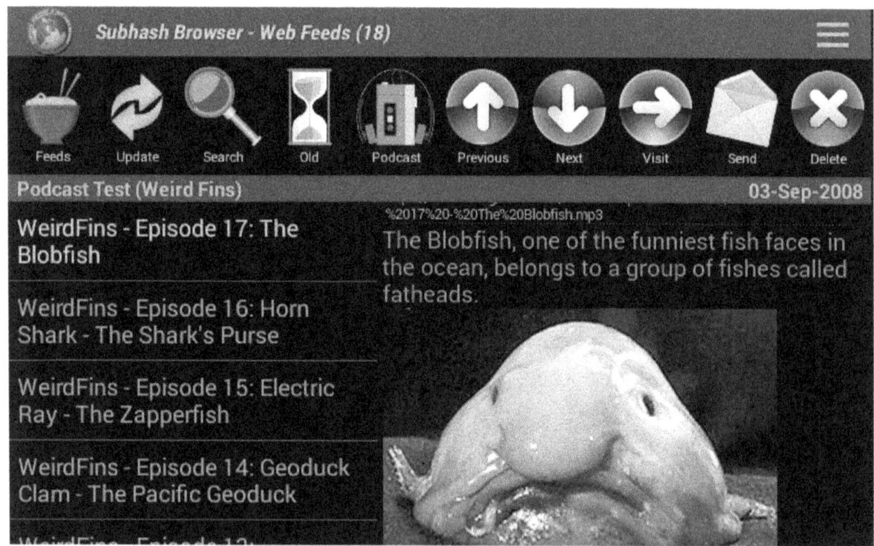

I have created a namesake Android browser app, which has a built-in RSS reader. This reader also supports title filters to reduce information overload. You can download it free from **www.VSubhash.in**.

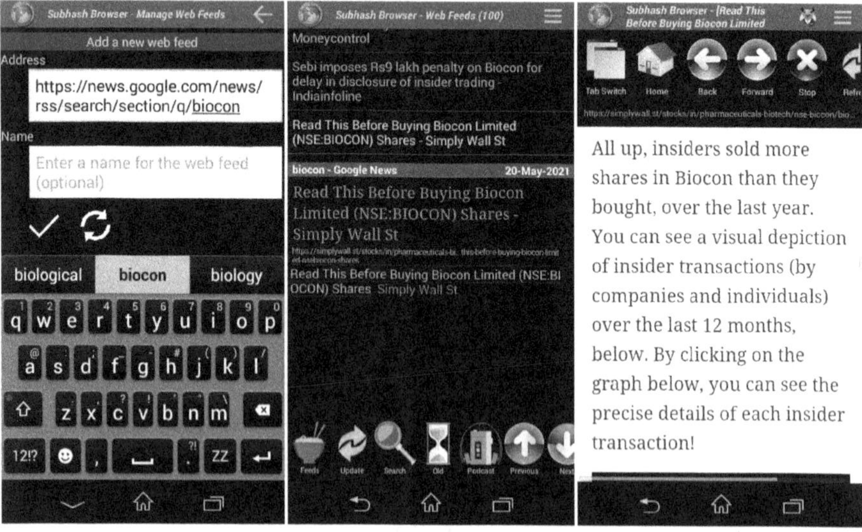

You can use the RSS feeds provided by news aggregators to track stocks. Suppose you want to track the stock of Biocon in the news, you can construct an

RSS feed like this:

```
https://news.google.com/news/rss/search/section/q/bio
con
```

For any other stock, just replace the last part of this URL with the stock's name. If the stock name has more than one word, you need to add a '+' symbol between the words and wrap the whole thing with a pair of '%22', which is code for quotation mark. If you want to track Reliance Industries, for example, change the URL like this:

```
https://news.google.com/news/rss/search/section/q/%22
reliance+industries%22
```

Websites advertise their RSS feeds using an orange icon. Look out for them and add their links to your RSS reader app. Some websites do not advertise their RSS feeds even though they provide them. In that case, you can use the RSS feed detector button in my app. If you are on a desktop browser, I suggest using my RSS-detecting browser script — you need to use it with the GreaseMonkey or TaperMonkey add-on.

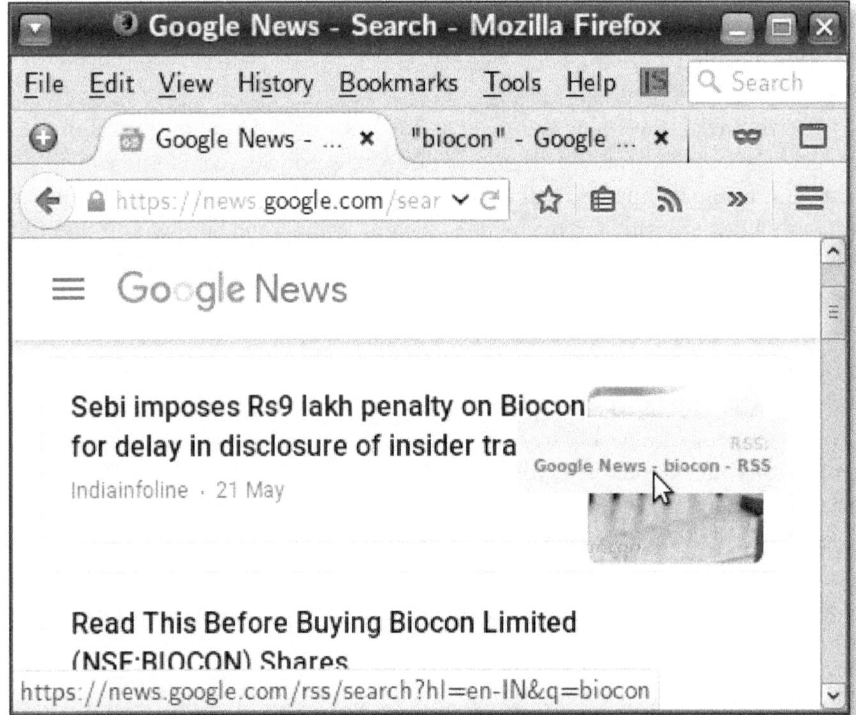

You can find the script at:

Time to buy

IPOs are a good time to buy shares. Financial newspapers do a good job of covering new IPOs. Always remember to read the author bio of the articles you read. It is important that they are not biased or have conflicts of interest. An extended stock crash is also a good time to fish for value. You may be able to pick good shares that were once overvalued. Do check why they were not able to withstand the crash. Stocks that remain stable or rise when there is carnage everywhere else should be good picks. They are more likely to better when times are good. **Invest a portion of your earning every month in stocks and bonds, as in other avenues such as gold or real estate. Spread your risks. Always have free cash for emergency needs. Slowly build a portfolio that will compound its earnings over time.**

Time to sell

How long should you hold a stock? When is the right time to sell? Any time is a right time to sell except when you follow the market to take part in a stampede to get out of the door. If you can make a profit from a sale, then it is a right time. If you can postpone a sale because there is a considerable upside in future, then that is fine too.

The financial news blog ZeroHedge in its title says 'On a long-enough timeline, the survival rate for everyone drops to zero.' Some companies will just disappear. Some companies will outlast you. But you are no good if you do not bequeath a decent portfolio to the next generation in your family. You do not have to consume it all while you are alive.

Do not let dips in the market to make you lose your nerve and sell at a loss. Wait it out. Unless your research suggests that a company is doomed or is set in a downward trajectory, do not sell early. Patience is a virtue. Many people in the market invest with borrowed money. They cannot wait for extended timelines. They have to sell at a loss to avoid a bigger loss in their borrowings. If you invest with your own money, you can afford to wait longer. If the company's business is sound and its future sits on solid fundamentals, then you can wait longer than the herd followers in the market.

You will find the following *stock investor anthem* in my book *2020 Fresh Clean Jokes For Everyone*. It is set to the tune of the nursery rhyme *Early to bed, early to rise*.

Early to invest
Early to sell
Ensures an investor retires in style

Market Movers

You may have read or heard about bulls and bears - brokers who push up share prices (bulls) or those who pummel them down (bears). They are market movers because they try to force the direction in which the market is moving. Brokers are not the only ones.

Like reading tea leaves...

What they teach you in school is only a foundation for what you will learn later in real life. It is with experience that you can make accurate predictions about the market.

In the 90s and early twenty-zeroes, I had a simple system to predict when the stockmarket would rise or go down. At that time, Foreign Institutional Investors (FIIs) had an outsized influence on the Indian stockmarket. Their funds were denominated in US dollar or some hard currency. The Indian rupee was very cheap (still is) compared to these foreign currencies. One US dollar or Sterling Pound could buy a lot of rupees. Whenever news spread that FIIs were interested in some Indian stock, its price would start to move up on the charts. Because the rise in the stock's price only had a marginal effect when converted back to dollars, FIIs would buy at whatever price the shares were offered. When some FII started selling some stock, its price would go down faster than usual. This was because these FIIs had a herd mentality. They did not have experienced or empowered staff in India. They blindly invested in stocks tracked by indexes maintained by large Wall Street firms such as Morgan Stanley. Rather than looking at the stockmarket, I would study the forex market reports and see if FIIs were buying or selling dollars there. If they were selling dollars, then they would be net buyers in the stockmarket over the next few weeks and the markets would definitely rise. If they were net buyers of dollars (to repatriate profits made in Indian rupees), I knew the market would go down soon. This system worked well for me for several years. When the *BusinessWorld* magazine had on its cover 'Bet your shirt on the market!', I knew it was not true. The market crashed, of course. Even the best people in the business can go wrong. Unless you develop your own knack for the market, you will only be following the herd.

My 'system' did not last. India's forex markets had grown tremendously on the back of Foreign Direct Investment (FDI), IT contracts to Indian tech companies and the continuing slide in the value of the rupee. Today, India has one of the biggest hoards of foreign currencies. The role of FIIs has diminished so much that forex reports do not even mention their activity. Indian Financial Institutions (FIs) have re-established their influence. Each year a mountain-load of money is invested in mutual funds and insurance plans by salaried taxpayers (for tax deductions) and the fund managers park this money in the stockmarket. This money is so big that stockmarket does not go down for anything. It is like a truck tyre filled with air that will not submerge for anything. Individual shares may go down but the market as a whole is resistant to a crash. Even the coronavirus pandemic did not bring it down. (Incidentally, I went to the city and bought a sovereign of gold for ₹30,000 when the lockdown was imposed in the US. As I write this, the price now is ₹36,600.)

FIIs are an example of how certain players in the market trigger directional movement across a broad swath of the market. FIIs are also testimony to how the influence of these players change over time. As an investor, you need to watch these market movers. In different markets, there are different market movers. In the US market, some large funds invest heavily the FANG stocks (Facebook, Amazon, Netflix and Google) irrespective of the returns. This sets the mood for the entire sector and IPOs in general. As long as the prices continue to rise, nobody's is complaining. When the party is over, there will be rivers of tears. As the bard of 2020 sang in the tune of 'Mary had a little lamb':

> FANG stocks are going down!
> Going down! Going down!
> FANG stocks are going down, taking the rest of the market!
>
> And, every bottom that FANG stocks hit!
> FANG stocks hit! FANG stocks hit!
> And, every bottom that FANG stocks hit, the rest of the market would reel around.

Rogue brokers

Sometimes, the market movers may be individual brokers. Harshad Mehta and Ketan Parekh had a God-like influence before they crashed the market at different times. I remember the moment outside the railway station when I saw *The Economic Times* headline that read something like *x years to the day, another bull crashes the market*. It was the same paper that gave these fraudsters a larger-than-life aura. Access to cheap bank funds had enabled these men to topple the market.

There are several ways that brokers try to manipulate shares. One of them is to create artificial demand. A broker buys a lot of shares of a particular script from the market. He borrows money using those shares as collateral. With that money, he buys even more shares. Others start noticing the demand and the price shoots up. After continuously wiping out supply in the market with such purchases and sending the share price to a high, the operator dumps the share in the market and makes a huge profit. Sometimes the rest of the market stops buying before the operator does. The broker then unloads his shares at a loss, which also causes a price crash.

Rogue government

There is no bigger influencer in the stockmarket than the Indian government. In countries with well-developed financial systems, the government does not interfere in the markets. (Theoretically, that is. Let us not kid ourselves.) The market takes care of itself, as they say. Oh, India is no rush to join that league. In the forex market, the **State Bank of India (SBI)** acts as the **Reserve Bank of India RBI**'s handmaiden to calm the markets. Goaded by the RBI, the SBI sells or buys dollars against it own interest. SBI does not have to worry because the central government covers its losses. The loser is of course the taxpayer. Given the self-defeating role that SBI plays, foreign banks such as Citibank and Bank of America make hundreds of millions (if not billions) at the expense of SBI.

'RBI has capacity to sell up to $30 b to halt rupee fall'

RBI may mobilise $20 b in NRI bonds

MUMBAI, DHNS: The Reserve Bank of India (RBI) has a capacity to sell up to $30 billion from its forex reserves to halt the arrest of depreciating rupee -- which breached an all-time low of Rs 60-mark against the dollar -- and for this, it may come out with an NRI bond issue to raise around $20 billion, said foreign brokerage Bank of America Merill Lynch here on Monday.

I have been tracking the Indian forex reserves for nearly three decades now. A strange thing I have seen is that India's foreign debt has always maintained parity its forex reserves. Whenever the reserves rise, Indian politicians and bureaucrats at the central and state governments seem to conspire to take out foreign loans to minimize any surplus. So, this mountain of foreign currencies that Indian government boasts about is no strength. In effect, the Indian taxpayer, from the poorest to the richest, is funding the fiscal (budget) and current account (forex) deficits of well-developed countries.

Another self-defeating operator is **Life Insurance Corporation of India (LIC)**. The Ministry of Finance makes the LIC to support the market when panic sets in. Panic sets in usually when FIIs are selling. Because FIIs are slow on the feet, sharp Indian brokers make fools of them. But, when the FIIs sell, they sell in droves. They will sell across the spectrum because they are stupid like that. (FIIs also sell in foreign markets to make up for losses in their home market.) My belief is that these FIIs pull some strings and the MoF orders LIC to buy up shares. LIC is also forced to buy shares that the government is selling as part of its disinvestment process. Every year, the fiscal deficit widens and the Indian government (goaded by foreign lenders such as IMF and World Bank) sells a portion of its holdings in government companies. When the market does not buy at the prices set by the government, guess who buys the shares? LIC.

CNBC anchor bemoans the fact that LIC was not there to save the market.

Before LIC, there was **Unit Trust of India (UTI)**, a big government-owned mutual fund. Because UTI is backed by the government, millions of Indian pensioners and salaried people blindly reposited their faith in the investment schemes of UTI. The MoF used to misuse UTI funds as it does now with LIC funds. It was not just the government - everyone from Harshad Mehta to Reliance Industries were exploiting UTI.

Rogue FIIs

Several decades ago, one FII (Morgan Stanley probably) was found trying to be artificially manipulating the value of some shares. What this FII did was to sell shares at below-market prices at regular intervals. This caused the shares of those unfortunate companies to fall. While the FII was banned from trading in a foreign country for price manipulation, it continues to do business in India. It even has a prestigious 'emerging markets' index that other FIIs blindly track.

Today, this sort of activity is specialized by **hedge funds**. A writer for MarketWatch opines in the wake of 2021 *GameStop* imbroglio:

> Hedge funds are essentially a conspiracy against their investors, who are variously known as 'limited partners,' 'clients' and 'total suckers,' depending on who is listening. The way hedge funds work: When the funds go up, the managers take a big chunk of the profits. When the funds go down, the clients eat the losses.

News factor

Apart from corporates and brokers, the news factor plays an important role in the market. If the rupee value falls, software companies will earn more rupees for every dollar they collect abroad. This will cause shares of IT companies to rise. If the government decreases the prices of controlled drugs, the shares prices of MNC (foreign or multinational company) pharma companies will fall.

Karma biting Apple

Nick Farrell   August 2015

Apple's problem is that it has nothing new to offer. Its business model was dependant on appearing to have the next important technology. While it usually borrowed this technology from someone else and marketed the hell out of it, it did a good job and managed to grow at a huge rate. It was helped by its legions of fanboys in the press, who would praise a plague rat if it had an Apple logo stitched on its behind.

Banking

Cash and other items of value form a company's assets. The money it owes others are its liabilities. For a bank, this is in reverse. Loans taken out by customers are assets. (This is why its bad loans portfolio is known as non-performing assets (NPAs).) The deposits created by its customers are its liabilities.

When a customer takes out a new loan, the bank merely updates his account with that money. They create new money just like that. They do not order a fresh batch of notes and coins. This is the reason growth in the economy is directly tied to new loans.

The central bank acts as a bank for banks. Ordinary banks can borrow from the central bank if they are not unable to enough of it from customers. The interest rate at which the central bank lends to domestic banks is known as the '**central bank rate**'. This is a benchmark rate for the lending system in the country. Banks align their lending and deposit rates with the *central bank rate* rate. (Deposit rates are lower than lending rate. The difference between these two rates brings most of their profits.) However, their own cost of funds and profit margin decides the ultimate bank lending rate. This is known by **Marginal Cost of Funds Based Lending Rate (MCLR)**. It is the minimum rate below which it will not lend. It is specified in percentage points where one point is equal to one percentage.

Banks can borrow cash from the central bank at the ' **repo rate**'. Banks may also deposit excess funds with the central bank and earn interest that way. The central bank's interest rate for these deposits is known as the 'reverse repo rate'. By adjusting these rates, the central bank can control the money supply, inflation and even the forex (foreign currency exchange) rate.

Currency, inflation and central bank

A quick lesson in economics might be due here. The RBI controls the interest rates in our country. The **central bank alters the interest rates to check inflation and the value of the nation's currency.**

Inflation means all-round price increases. This is because too much money chases too few goods. To reduce inflation, the RBI increases the interest rates. The amount of money in circulation then comes down as borrowing money from banks and financial institutions is costlier and putting money in banks becomes advantageous. As the economy is drained of its excess money supply, there is less money going after commodities and prices come down. Effectively, inflation comes down.

The RBI will also increase interest rates (borrowing/deposit rates) when the value of the rupee goes down against foreign currencies. This can happen when supply of foreign currency to India falls. More Indian rupees are spent to acquire the scarcer foreign currency to pay for imports. When interest rates rise, rupees are driven from the hands of the people into the banking system. When the market finds itself with fewer rupees, there is less money to spend on foreign currencies and they become cheaper (Indian rupee rises).

In the late 90s, the Indian rupee was falling against the dollar and the RBI increased interest rates. At that time, IDBI offered bonds at the prevailing interest rates. Wonder how much? 14%! I asked my father to invest in these bonds and he never again got to invest in such high-yield bonds. Opportunities like that arise only once in several decades.

However, when interest rates increase, banks will find it difficult to give out loans. This has a macroeconomic effect of constraining growth. This, in turn, affects the stockmarket. Alternatively, a low-interest rate regime fuels speculation and the creation of market bubbles. Interest rates are a double-edged sword.

Another truth about the economy is that **commodity prices are determined by export prices**. Local prices for commodities usually reflect the prices they can fetch in the export market. For example, take the tea prices. India is one of the largest producers of tea. Yet, we pay international prices for it. Nobody is going to sell you tea cheap if people outside the country are ready to buy them at higher rates. This is one reason why Indians spend most of their income on food. In the US, on the contrary, food expenses are very small and most of a person's income is spent on repaying mortgage on his car or house — a reason why they have more material comforts than us.

Government rules and regulations

Apart from economic fundamentals, government policies such as taxation, price controls, etc., affect a company's fortunes. People who have advance knowledge on such price—altering information will try to take advantage of such situations. Promoters or officials of a company might be privy to information that can have an effect on the share price. They might use it to their advantage by buying or selling shares themselves or by giving it to operators in the market.

When a company takes up an expensive modernization drive or obtains large loans, it will not be able to provide huge returns in the near future. In such cases, their prices can take a dive. Alternatively, when they are on the verge of completing the exercise and their investments start to pay off, the share prices go up.

Even in the middle of the coronavirus pandemic, the stocks of companies making disinfectants and hospital consumables have gone up. Government-imposed lockdowns have helped the share prices of online e-commerce and video-streaming outfits.

Summary

There are winners and losers in every situation. As an investor, you can make money on both.

The world

Stockmarkets do not operate in isolation. They are affected by things that happen in their home country and abroad.

USA

The United States is the biggest economy in the world. It is the home of some of the biggest corporations in the world. It exports and imports all kinds of things and this trade forms a major part of international commerce. Their government, neither at the national or state level, own any industry. (Not true.) Almost everything is left to private enterprise. (Not true.) For instance, the US does not have a nationwide network of railways because the central government never thought of putting a national railway network. Any railways that were built came into existence thanks to private industrialists. To travel across long distances, most Americans use their cars if they cannot do it by plane. Almost every aspect of the American life is commercialised and every opportunity is exploited. For example, an American family will eat its breakfast out of the fridge or food cupboard. An entire breakfast can be made packaged milk and cereal boxes. Every food item is processed. Almost every part of the economy is underwritten by some sort of insurance. If the United States is the most litigious nation in the world, it is in part because of insurance. A big reason for the high productivity of American people is the use of tools. They have tools for every type of activity. If something does not have a tool, then it is probably not worth doing. A sizeable section of the populace consists of old people. An American youth typically leaves his home once his education is finished and fends for himself. The parents similarly do not depend on their children in later life. Most of them get into retirement homes or make arrangements to that effect. They hold a lot of funds in the stockmarket. They are steady customers for insurance and healthcare industries. Though the US has the largest number of publications, most Americans do not read newspapers. They get all their news from a few big news conglomerations. The office of the American President gets a surprisingly high amount of coverage in the news. If their President gets a colonoscopy, it will be the top news and they will cover it considerable detail while everyone is having breakfast.

Like many other things, American politicians have gone ahead and institutionalised corruption. They do not like to use the term bribery and instead prefer the euphemism *lobbying*. Vested interests can line the pockets of politicians legally. Typically, an industry group like the tech industry or the arms industry would pay a few millions as campaign contributions in exchange for billions of dollars in tax breaks or subsidies or rule changes. The influence of corporates is so powerful that they can make the US go to war or indulge in civil war, assassinations or genocide in Third−World countries. There is little that

American people can do to solve the problem. America is addicted to war. Like in India, the cancer of corruption has taken over vital functions of the government that it is not possible to remove it without killing the whole.

An example of how private interest groups can derail public interest is how the Obama administration talked a big game about 'Climate Change' and then allowed oil drilling in the Arctic... for a foreign company. Such things happen because the US is a Fascist state. It has passed so many laws that it has neatly transitioned from a democratic country to a Fascist state.

Only a stooge of the globalist kleptocracy can become the US president. The late actor Peter Sellers is best known for his *Pink Panther* movies but his masterpiece was the adaptation of Jersy Kosinski's *Being There*. In this novel, a mentally stunted man becomes the US president through a series of unexpected events. His childishly simple answers and calm demeanour is mistaken for genius. With some new but powerful friends, he ends up in the White House. The reaction of his former Black caretaker is priceless.

> Gobbledegook! All the time he talked gobbledegook! An' it's for sure a White man's world in America. Hell, I raised that boy since he was the size of a pissant an' I'll say right now he never learned to read an' write. No, sir! Had no brains at all… was stuffed with rice puddin' between the ears! Short-changed by the Lord and dumb as a jackass an' look at him now! Yes, sir, all you gotta be is white in America an' you get whatever you want! Just listen to that boy — gobbledegook!

I saw this movie when George W. Bush became president and I could not but notice the strong resemblance. Fact, indeed, is stranger than fiction!

It's time to give the elites a bigger say in choosing the pr...

www.washingtonpost.com/opinions/2020/02/18/fix-primaries-let-elites-dec

Recall how the ~~retarded~~ lexically challenged George W Bush, with his permanent smirk, was supposed to have degrees from Harvard and Yale? The American kleptocracy chooses such extremely dumb individuals as presidential candidates so they can be surrounded with advisors and minders who actually call the shots. They tell the sock puppets when to smile and what script to read. But, the baseline is that they are all idiots. Their past is most likely fiction. The world's greatest teleprompter actor Obama claimed to be a constitutional lawyer... (and was questioned by the Clinton campaign. Let's forget that.)

The latest globalist protégé is Alexandria Ocasio Cortez, the congresswoman from Queens, NY. A.k.a. AOC, she is supposed to be an economics graduate but does not know the three different branches of government or the difference between Keynes and Friedman. But, when a people's champion and a rank outsider like Donald Trump becomes the US president, the gloves come off. The kleptocrats bare their fangs and show their true colours.

Next to UK, the US is the world's best shadow Orwellian state. Americans are so blissfully unaware of it that they get offended when they are told that their country is Fascist and it is coaxing other countries to imitate its tyrannical and exploitative policies through globalisation.

Is the Gates Foundation Still Investing in Private Prisons?

Bill and Melinda Gates' philanthropy won't say.

Bill Gates speaks at a UN conference on polio eradication. John Minchillo/AP.

When someone from the ruling class commits a major crime, there is no investigation. (I did not say Hunter Biden's laptop or Hillary Clinton's BlackBerries.) When an average Joe commits a minor infraction, he gets thrown in the clink for decades.

More than one-third of American Black male population has been in jail or will be in jail. The high delinquency rates among the Black population is because most of the men are feedstock for the prison-industrial complex. Alleged philanthropists like Bill Gates and Warren Buffet are big investors in private prisons. Many police forces are not government employees but private unions on contract with the local government. Their salaries are inflated using civil-asset forfeiture laws, which do not require conviction to seize assets. After Bush and Obama administrations provided military-style weapons to civilian police forces, SWAT raids for minor infractions became more common. In general, most policemen are poorly trained but are armed with guns. They shoot first and ask questions later.

US dollar

The US dollar is the global reserve currency. All other countries need to hold a reserve of this currency because much of world's trade, particularly the crucial petroleum trade, is conducted in US dollars. Even countries with free floating currency (hard currencies whose values are determined by the market and not controlled/restricted by their central bank) have to acquire US dollars to pay for such imports. While countries with free-floating currencies can easily exchange their currency for the dollar, countries with soft currencies (mostly developing countries) have work hard to acquire the US dollar. They do this with exports, tourism and sometimes borrowing. In contrast, the US just prints the currency. It does not have to create anything of value to create the dollar. It is a unique privilege of having the global reserve currency and a powerful military. This is the unofficial reason why the US invades any country that switches from the US dollar to the Euro or gold. The official reason could be anything from terrorism to weapons of mass destruction to human rights. Read my book *American Foreign Policy For Dummies* for more information.

In 2005, an economics savant wrote in a blog post titled *Lose The Dollar*:

> In The Devil's Dictionary by Ambrose Bierce, an alliance is defined as the union of two thieves who have their hands so deeply inserted in each other's pocket they cannot separately plunder a third. The situation with the dollar is similar to that. The fortunes of Japan and China are so deeply wedded to the American economy that they are unlikely to dump the dollar in a flash. But, things are so bad that the dollar will crash even if there is no diversification i.e., it will crash if either central bank stops its purchase of American treasury bonds. Strangely, if the U.S. dollar does crash, the American economy will not be the one that is most affected. Surprised?
>
> When you owe a bank a thousand dollars, the bank owns you. When you owe the bank a billion dollars, you own the bank. If the US Federal Reserve goes bust, then central banks holding American treasury bonds will have no option but to recycle American money into toilet paper, much like what Russia did with the Soviet Rouble. And, we in the Third World have the most to suffer because governments never go bankrupt; they force others into bankruptcy.

Another strange thing about the US is that its central bank is not owned by the government. It is notionally owned by a nationwide group of *federal reserve banks* that are in turn are owned by private banks. The *Federal Reserve Bank of New York* (the **New York Fed**) owns most of the voting shares and is the real decision maker and its representation in the Federal Reserve board holds all the cards. In a 2009 suit filed by a Bloomberg reporter (who wanted to know how the $2 trillion Wall Street bailout ('lending program') was spent), the New York Fed stated that it was not a public institution and did not have to release 'trade secrets'. (Bloomberg; April 2009; *Fed Shrouding $2 Trillion in Bank Loans in*

'Secrecy,' Suit Says]. Although the Federal Reserve governor is appointed by the US president, he is not answerable to any public official.

Quantitative easing (money printing)

One of the reasons for having a private and independent central bank was supposedly to prevent a profligate government (or a ruthless king) from printing currency like crazy. Globalist kleptocracy fought hard to bring both the government and the central bank under its control but it is the one that is now addicted to money printing. The US Federal Reserve has greatly expanded its balance sheet by printing money. This money is given at no interest to a select few Wall Street banks who then lend it to other banks and institutions and even the government (when they purchase government securities) at interest.

The US kleptocracy makes a lot of money from the stockmarket so it does not allow it correct (burst the bubble). The US Federal Reserve through the New York Fed operates a *Plunge-Protection Team*. This team buys up shares of private companies(!) to prevent a correction in the market.

> The stockmarket is falling down!
> Falling down! Falling down!
> The stockmarket is falling down!
> Dear Plunge-Protection Team, are you listening!
>
> Stop inflating financial bubbles!
> Financial bubbles! Financial bubbles!
> Stop inflating financial bubbles!
> Dear Federal Reserve, isn't it a moral hazard!
>
> Gold and silver are also manipulated!
> Manipulated! Manipulated!
> Gold and silver are also manipulated!
> Dear Austrian economists, there is just not enough to go around!
>
> — Set to the tune of *London bridge is falling down*

Central Banks buying stocks is an anachronism. But, it makes wealthy Wall Street investors more wealthy so there! For a government that spent more than half a century fighting Socialism and Communism abroad, intervening in the market and propping up the stockmarket does not seem to be contradictory at all. **Fascism, Socialism and Communism all concentrate power in the hands of a few while depriving it from the masses.**

It is not just the US Federal Reserve that is buying up the stockmarket. The EU central bank has done the same and so has Japan's. In fact, the central bank is the biggest investor in all three markets. This is extremely shameful and unprecedented but it goes on. The US, EU and Japanese central banks are even buying corporate deposits! **The US Federal Reserve does not know what to buy that (in 2020) they appointed the fund manager BlackRock to handle purchases for them!** It is like giving a six-year-old kid a $1000 dollars so that he can buy all the candy he wants.

Gold

When the markets are in turmoil, investors seek safety in gold. During the 2011-12 debt crisis, several European countries were on the verge of defaulting on their debt. The price of gold started rising. In 2013, a worldwide media blitzkrieg attacking gold was led by Wall Street firm Goldman Sachs. Gold was out, they said. It was a barbarous relic, they said. Meanwhile, the Bank of International Settlements (BIS) had quietly amended the Basel 3 bank liquidity rules replacing gold with stocks! The coordinated attack depressed gold for a while but the coronavirus pandemic and the worldwide lockdown is threatening to bring it back. (All this talk about cryptocurrencies and such, I believe, is to prevent a return to gold in times of crisis.) Most central banks have emptied their gold vaults. Some say they have gold but not a lot of people trust them.

In a strange case, the US Federal Reserve admitted that it had melted 'some' of the gold that Germany had left with them for safe storage.

This is small part of a bigger illustration at VisualCapitalist.com

Where's Germany's Gold

Almost half of Germany's gold is stored in vaults under the streets in Manhattan. Or, is it?

February 2015, Bloomberg: … "The organisational preparations were very time-consuming since the required agreements and contracts are voluminous and detailed," the Bundesbank's Thiele said in a statement four weeks later. Additionally, some bars in New York had to be melted and recast. To Boehringer, the recasting was the ultimate red flag. It meant any trace of original serial numbers had been wiped out. "Their untouched existence since the 1960s is no longer provable," Boehringer says.

The Bundesbank explained that it recast the bars because they hadn't met the "London good delivery" standard. Such gold is at least 99.5 percent pure and comes in bars of roughly 400 troy ounces, or 12.44 kilograms. They must bear certain marks, such as year of manufacture, and have sides that measure within specified dimensions. The gold in American vaults is a mix of London good delivery and lower-quality bars. Boehringer figured maybe the German bars had oddball weights and purities and needed to be recast.

He did some quick math on the Bundesbank's own numbers, dividing the total weight it had disclosed for New York holdings by the number of bars it listed. It came out to about 12.5 kilograms per bar—same as London good delivery. If the central bank's published numbers were right, Boehringer says, "There would not be a reason to melt them, but they did."…

Here is a gold investor anthem (set to the tune of *Eeny, meeny, miny, moe*) that I wrote for my jokebook.

> Markets boom and markets crash
> Always have some barbarous relic in your hands
> Even when your government files for bankruptcy
> Gold is nobody's liability

Low/Zero/Negative Interest Rates

Wall Street Socialism requires a lot of money and low interest rates. No wonder that the US has had near-zero interest rates for more than a decade. Ditto for EU and Japan. There is so much money in the banking system that several banks are charging customers interest for depositing money with them. This, in effect, is a form of negative interest rates. With true negative interest rates, bank will have to pay interest to those who take out a loan!

> Negative interest rates! Negative interest rates
> Do you take me for a fool?
> With negative interest rates!
>
> If I lend one dollar, then I lose some cents!
> Do you take me for a fool?
> With negative interest rates!
>
> — Set to the tune of *Hot Cross Buns*

Europe

Western Europe consists of several developed countries with functioning democracies. Their populations are small and their productivity is high. Together, they have formed the European Union. The EU is now a huge trading block and its common currency (the Euro) provides some competition to the dollar as an alternative reserve currency. Unfortunately, it has greatly expanded its bureaucracy and has it own complement of voluminous laws and regulations.

Instead of being a nimble union that could compete with the US in size, the EU is projected as a superstate that could be replicated in other parts of the world to ultimately form a world government. The EU was started as a common market, then as a customs union and now a currency union.

The EU is also run by kleptocrats. It has been printing the Euro like crazy and buying up falling markets (shares and bonds). Its impending failure is being blamed by the lack of a fiscal union. A fiscal union is where the constituent nations conceded their sovereignty and the EU decides the government budgets as well. As it is, the EU is extremely undemocratic. There is an EU parliament. It has no power create or modify legislation. That power is given to a unelected cronies appointed by the heads of governments from each member state. Fortunately, the UK has quit the EU. However, Scotland wants to remain in the EU. UK's opposition party the Labour Party also wants to get back, even though it has been defeated in subsequent elections.

Much of Eastern Europe was previously under the Soviet umbrella. After the disintegration of the Soviet Union, most of them have become independent though the democracies that they have established are not free of Western interference. Many of them today are part of NATO and look up to the West primarily for funds and notionally for protection against the mythical Russian invasion. For its part, Russia has done well since the breakup though initially it suffered under Yeltsin (who was a thorough Western stooge). Most of Russia's current fortunes are from the sale of oil and gas rather than substantial industrial development. Russia has the capability to become the most powerful country in the world considering the resources it has but the West will never allow it.

Russia is an Eurasian country. There are several countries in Europe and Asia that have lived under its shadow since Tsarist times. Quite a few of them are in Central Asia. They are rich in oil, gas and other minerals, and have great strategic value. Russia, the West and lately China compete with each other for influence there.

US vs. Russia vs. Europe

During the Clinton years, the US tried to build gas pipelines from Central

Asia to Europe. British Petroleum was the lead investor in it but the US was expending its diplomatic/military/intelligence resources fighting for it. (Why should the US work for a British company? Is it George Soros?)

The US poured billions of dollars into countries like Poland, Ukraine, Georgia, Yugoslavia (broken up) and other Eastern European countries and turned them into anti-Russian satellites. The funds of US Department of State were routed through NGOs such as George Soros' Freedom House, the Republican party's International Republican Institute (IRI) and the Democratic party's National Democratic Institute (NDI) into these countries to ~~bribe~~ 'educate' journalists, ~~stooges~~ politicians and 'activists' about democracy. Despite

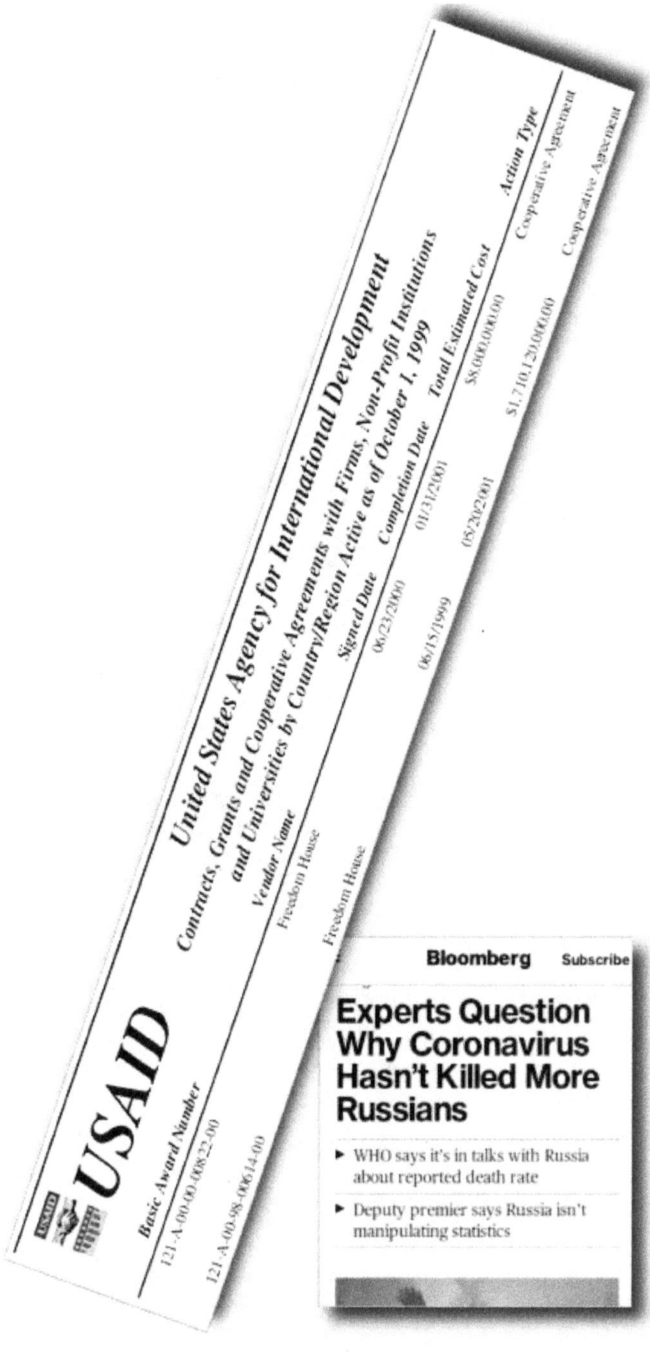

USAID

United States Agency for International Development

Contracts, Grants and Cooperative Agreements with Firms, Non-Profit Institutions and Universities by Country/Region Active as of October 1, 1999

Vendor Name	Basic Award Number	Signed Date	Completion Date	Total Estimated Cost	Action Type
Freedom House	121-A-00-00-00835-00	06/23/2000	01/31/2001	$8,000,000.00	Cooperative Agreement
Freedom House	121-A-00-98-00614-00	06/15/1999	05/28/2001	$1,710,120,000.00	Cooperative Agreement

Bloomberg Subscribe

Experts Question Why Coronavirus Hasn't Killed More Russians

▶ WHO says it's in talks with Russia about reported death rate

▶ Deputy premier says Russia isn't manipulating statistics

American efforts, Russia's Gazprom and other state-owned enterprises managed to build their own pipelines to customers in several countries in Europe.

In recent years, the US has become a net oil exporter instead of being a net importer thanks to the boom in their shale industry. However, this industry is floating on a sea of debt and is expected to suffer devastating bankruptcies in the coming years. It is for this reason that US has been placing sanctions after sanctions on Russia while trying to create a market for its natural gas producers in Europe.

The Americas

The rest of the Americas (except for Canada) is made up of mainly of developing countries. Most of the wealth in these countries continues to be owned by landed gentry from Europe or megacorporations from the US. After World War II, the interests of these companies were threatened by numerous Left−leaning

≡ **The New York Times** 

CIA Says It Used Nicaraguan Rebels Accused of Drug Tie

July 17, 1998

The Central Intelligence Agency continued to work with about two dozen Nicaraguan rebels and their supporters during the 1980's despite allegations that they were trafficking in drugs, according to a classified study by the C.I.A.

...

The C.I.A.'s decision to classify this second volume has already been met with criticism in Congress. Senator John Kerry, Democrat of Massachusetts, who led a 1987 Congressional inquiry into allegations of contra drug connections, wrote a letter Thursday to the Director of Central Intelligence, George J. Tenet, asking that the report be immediately declassified.

...

"Some of us in Congress at the time, in 1985, 1986, were calling for a serious investigation of the charges, and C.I.A. officials did not join in that effort," Mr. Kerry said. "There was a significant amount of stonewalling. I'm afraid that what I read in the report documents the degree to which there was a lack of interest in making sure the laws were being upheld."

movements (Commies) that seemed to enjoy popular support. (The grass is greener on the other side.) The US would then, under the guise of fighting Communism, create armed insurgencies or engineer coups or rig elections or unleash false propaganda in these countries. To finance these activities a lot of money was needed, not all of which was met by the American taxpayer. Hence, illicit drugs were manufactured in these countries and sold in the US and Western Europe. These drug syndicates were protected by shady government organizations like the CIA.

While people in the West were getting addicted to drugs, hundreds of thousands of Latin Americans were getting killed or tortured or disappearing without a trace. When an American protégé has been firmly established in power, a pogrom of killings, torture and reprisals would follow. Schools, hospitals, homes, churches, etc., were not spared. Today, sorry excuses for democracy exist in these countries. Foreigners or their clients continue to own most of the wealth. People are still getting killed and tortured. The death squads and secret police continue to exist. Democracy and dissent continue to be suppressed. And the all−important drug businesses continue to flourish. The US provides these countries with "aid" in the form of weapons and equipment. When this aid is not used to put down dissent, it is used to combat drug syndicates that are competing with those run by the US. The rulers of these countries serve the interests of the United States rather than that of their people. If there had been any history of independent or democratic rule, they have only been overthrown. While most Americans believes that their country stands for freedom and democracy, the US government's policies abroad is driven by private interests. Many of these South American countries are rich in minerals. The political and economic fortunes of these countries affect the prices of the minerals or the commodities they produce and in turn affect world markets.

Chicago Tribune

EX-DEA-AGENT: CIA DRUG ~~SALES~~SMUGGLING AIDED CONTRAS

By **Dave Harmon, McAllen Monitor, Knight-Ridder/Tribune**

JANUARY 26, 1993 | MCALLEN, TEXAS

A former U.S. drug agent based in Central America says the covert U.S. operation that supplied arms to the Nicaraguan contras also smuggled drugs into the United States to help finance the war against the leftist Sandinista government.

Celerino "Cele" Castillo III of McAllen, a former agent of the Drug Enforcement Administration, said an investigation he conducted while based in Guatemala in the mid-1980s revealed that the Central Intelligence Agency and former National Security Council staffer Oliver North operated two hangars from Ilopango Air Force Base in El Salvador.

Castillo said airplanes operating from the hangars delivered narcotics to the U.S. and the Bahamas and brought back cash to finance the supply operation.

Castillo, 43, said that when he reported the activity, he met a wall of resistance from the CIA, the U.S. ambassador to El Salvador and his own agency. He said he has come forward out of frustration

Africa

Much of Africa, similarly, is rich in minerals. Western companies provide funds to armed groups to gain control of these resources. Sometimes, the group that had taken money and realised their objectives no longer remains loyal to its patron. So, the foreign companies start financing another group and the fighting continues. Millions die in such civil wars and genocides. If any of these Third World countries has a decent military, the Western companies pay off the generals to prevent any politician from usurping their investments. No real democracy can grow in these countries. Whenever you hear or read that some fighting is going on in an African country, try to find out what mineral that country produces or which companies do business there and which industries will be affected by supply shortfalls.

Asia

In the mid−90s, an American company (Unocal) tried to build a gas pipeline to India from a Central Asian country via Afghanistan and Pakistan. Though the country in question was ready, Afghanistan remained in total anarchy. With generous help from the US, UK, Saudi Arabia, and other countries, this company raised a huge army of "religious students" (*Taleban*) from Pakistan and invaded Afghanistan and established a much−hated totalitarian regime. The Western press still puts out fiction that the group was created to fight the USSR, which had occupied Afghanistan previously, but in reality the group came up overnight only to fight native Afghan warlords, who had carved out individual fiefdoms out of country, long after the Russians had left. The Taliban created a government that was based on a primitive interpretation of Islam, intentionally so, to deflect or suppress any criticism of being a Western setup. They sheltered Osama and allegedly caused the 9/11 WTC attacks. They survived the US bombardment but could not stop the Afghan Mujahideen who swooped into Kabul with Russian help. The Russians were enemies no more but the US managed to establish their stooge in power. The Taliban regrouped with some of their former enemies and continue to hold sway over parts of Afghanistan. They are supported by Pakistan and are all set to come back to power once NATO forces leave.

Although India was supposed to be the market for this Central Asian gas, it has developed its own and foreign supplies in the meantime. The entire Afghan misadventure was a waste of money but brought colossal profits for arms companies and private military contracts. War is good for Wall Street.

The most economical way out for Central Asian gas is through Russia. As war raged and waned in Afghanistan, Russia laid several pipelines and developed markets in Europe. The whole Russia obsession during the Trump/Obama/Bush years are a continuing saga for the control of gas producers, distribution and markets.

Asia has several other places where conflicts have risen in the scramble for control of mineral wealth. If in Afghanistan religion was used as a cover to deflect criticism, in East Timor religion was used to divide people. Today, companies from Australia and the West exploit East Timor while the people continue to wallow in poverty. Similar takeovers were attempted in other parts of Indonesia after the Western stooge Suharto died. (He overthrew the popularly elected Sokerno and instituted a reign of terror.)

In Sri Lanka, rebellion was stoked by the West among the Tamils living in the northern part of the island nation. The armed outfit LTTE murdered all of its opponents and projected itself as the sole representative of Sri Lankan Tamils. During the prolonged civil war, the LTTE collected funds in Western countries and important terrorists were given asylum there. But, the LTTE failed to break up Sri Lanka. Finally, the US asked Sri Lankan government to start negotiating with LTTE. When the LTTE failed to make peace, Sri Lanka was given the go-ahead for an all-out war against the LTTE. The LTTE was defeated and its notorious leader was killed. However, several important functionaries including hitmen and arms smugglers were given asylum in Western countries, despite the fact that among LTTE's assassination victims were two prime ministers - India's Rajiv Gandhi and Sri Lanka's Premadasa. Sri Lanka finally reconciled with the people in the North and the island is peaceful again. Unfortunately, it has now been pushed into the orbit of China and has fallen into a debt trap thanks to a few white-elephant infrastructure projects.

China

China is one of the few remaining Communist countries. It was a big kingdom for several hundred years. In the 19th century, the opium trade by East India Company and the subsequent *Opium Wars* weakened the monarchy. China was then carved into spheres of influence by European imperial powers and Japan. Nationalists led by Chiang Kai-shek tried to overthrow these invaders but he was betrayed by the United

States who supported the Communists led by Mao. Their grouse was that Kai-shek would not sign an agreement for handing over the reins of Chinese economy (after independence) to US capitalists. (This was standard procedure in South America under the US *hemispheric norms*.) With Western help, the Communists routed the Nationalists who fled to Formosa (Taiwan). The

Communists established themselves on the mainland. Millions died under Mao's *Cultural Revolution* and his artificial famines. (Mainland Chinese began eating anything and everything that moves because of these famines.) Religion was banned and traditions were lost. China occupied Tibet and replaced most of the local population with Han Chinese people. Hong Kong and Macao remained under UK and Portugal but returned to Chinese control (the leases ran out). Hong Kong, under Western management, had by then developed into a huge trading hub. Its foreign currency reserves were almost as big as China's until recently. China treats Hong Kong as a special administrative region (SAR) and rules it by decree. Hong Kong now finds increased competition from mainland cities like Shanghai.

China and several East Asian countries have been on a modernization drive for a few decades and have established infrastructure and investment facilities on the lines of developed countries. This has led to a great deal of investments in their economies. Unfortunately, most of what these countries manufacture are exported. When China devalued its currency in 90s, the rest of East Asia plunged into crisis. This was because the Chinese worker was the cheapest of them all. A Chinese worker will work 7 days a week on low pay and practically make no complaints or demands. Few East Asians countries could compete with that. In fact, no worker in any country can compete with a Chinese quasi-slave.

Exploited workers are one of the first ones to fall for Communist/Socialist propaganda but few of them realise that in workers' unions are banned in a Communist state.

Oil

Oil is the backbone of the world economy. The number of countries that produce it is small but all the countries in the world consume it. Though United States produces a lot of oil, its economy is so big that its own production is not enough. (Lately, it has become oil surplus thanks to the shale oil boom. It continues to forage oil abroad and subvert nation states.)

The OPEC (Organisation of Petroleum Exporting Countries) is a cartel of oil producers and they have for long fixed the price of oil. Lately, Russia has been producing and exporting large quantities of oil and this has lessened the hold of OPEC on oil prices. Most of the oil comes from the Middle East. These countries are monarchies and police states. Almost all of them are unified in their hate for Israel though their official position may be different. ~~Israel, no doubt, lives in a tough neighbourhood and it is a credit to their perseverance that have held on to their small land for so long.~~

The real story behind Israel is rarely told to a Western audience. The Roman empire expelled all Jews out of Palestine. Except for Christians and another small Jewish tribe, all Jews had to leave. These people spread and settled all over the Middle East. Most of the Jews living today are descendants of an Eastern Russian ethnic minority that converted to Judaism. They are known as *Ashkenazi Jews* and have no relation to Palestine. The original Jews of Palestine are known as *Sephardic Jews*. With the discovery of oil in the Middle East, the Jewish Rothschild family became involved in the fate of Jews, much to their detriment. A Jewish colony in Palestine (Zionism) was planned. By this time, Arabs had settled in Palestine and had been living there close to two millennia. Despite a lot of financial inducements, Jews were only trickling into Palestine. Even when Hitler made life difficult for Jews, not many turned to Palestine. They preferred to move to countries neighbouring Germany. Hitler and Fascism was supported overtly and covertly by Western financial and industrial circles. (Read *Wall Street and the rise of Hiter* by Prof. Anthony Sutton.) Zionist organization also collaborated with Nazi Germany for emigration into Palestine while they lobbied Western countries to close their borders to fleeing Jews. Later, Nazi Germany occupied several countries in which Jews had sought refuge. Jews were hunted down and brought back to concentration camps in Germany. The best among them were picked for Palestine. Jewish numbers in Palestine swelled. In 1947, when Palestine was illegally divided by the United Nations at the behest of the major powers and without the consent of Arabs living there, Jews got 67% of the land when they owned only 7% of it. European Jews, who formed 33% of the population (swelled by refugee arrivals) got away with more than two-thirds of their host country. Israel later occupied most of the rest of the land and also expelled Arabs out of their land.

In fact, Israel has done so well that they now illegally hold parts of Syria and Lebanon. Israel has much to thank the United States, particularly its Jewish constituent, for their success. Jews in America have done well. They are an industrious lot. They look out for one another. They are really not big on equal opportunity employment. They own most of the businesses and media there. An example of their power is the fact that any movie about the Jewish Holocaust will win an Oscar if it is part of the nominations. American politicians cannot anger the Jews by taking a tough position on Israel. Anyone criticizing Israel will be immediately branded a Nazi. If the criticism manages to overcome that opposition, then they hold up pictures of Hitler and the Holocaust, no matter how much hate and destruction Israel bears up on the people of Palestine. Jewish organizations visit schools, colleges, government offices and even private organizations to spread propaganda about the evils of 'anti-Semitism'. The word *semitic* refers to all Middle Easterners but Jews have co-opted the name for themselves. Of late, their tactics have been picked by other minorities. Blacks and non-Whites pretend to persecuted by Whites and wreak vengeance on anyone they do not like. Several churches and synagogues have been firebombed and attacked but it does not matter anymore because Jews are now lumped together with Whites.

The situation in the Middle East cannot get any better because there are many parties in Israel and there is a race for political brinkmanship to take the toughest position on Palestine. Every time the situation in the Middle East goes wrong, the oil prices tend go north and stock prices tend to go south.

Commodity markets

Thankfully, the Middle East produces only oil. Some of our other needs are handled by commodity markets. Commodity exchanges are markets that deal with items like tea, coffee, sugar, etc. The **Chicago Board of Trade (CBOT)** is a good example of a commodity market. The **London Metal Exchange (LME)** is another commodity market. It deals with metals like copper, aluminium, etc.

Bullion markets

When production of minerals or agricultural commodities are affected by adverse political or environmental events, it can immediately drive up the price of the commodities. This is not the case with gold and silver (precious metals - bullion), as trading in these two metals is dominated by paper trading (no-delivery contracts). The paper gold and silver contracts are almost totally delinked from supply and demand changes. The US mint could run out of supply and London warehouses could be empty but the bullion markets would act as if nothing was amiss. Several big banks (bullion banks) have been convicted for bullion price manipulation (Forbes; 2019; 'Yes, Gold Is Being Manipulated. But To What Extent?'). Several central banks are rumoured to have lent all their gold stocks to these banks and are under-reporting their bullion reserves.

There are gold ETFs (exchange traded funds) that claim to hold the metal in their warehouses on behalf of investors. Do not invest in gold ETFs, as the market is so badly manipulated and you do not want suffer counterparty risk. Stocks held by ETFs could also be seized by the government when they become bankrupt. If you want to invest in gold, buy the metal and hold it in your personal bank locker. Buy only 24-carat gold (pure gold). If you want to buy gold as jewellery, buy 22-carat jewellery (2 carats copper). Do not buy low-quality gold (14-16 carats) that US stores typically sell.

Currency markets

The currency market essentially revolves around the world. It runs 24 hours of the day. When a market closes in one part of the world, it opens in another. Until a few decades ago, the currency values were determined by the amount of gold reserves that a country had. In the 70s, French President Charles de Gualle sent a destroyer to New York harbour and shipped back their gold. Subsequently, Nixon administration removed the god peg and let it float freely on the international market. Given that oil trade is settled in dollars, there would always be a demand for dollar. Today, currencies of most developed nations float freely. Currencies of most developing countries are tightly controlled by their central banks. When a central bank places several restrictions on currency conversion, they have a soft currency. When there are no controls, it floats freely in the international market on the basis of supply and demand. It can be converted to other currencies without first gaining permission of the central bank. Such currencies are called hard currencies. Developing countries with free floats or loose controls can become targets of speculative attacks, as happened in the East Asian financial crisis of the late 90s.

Multinationals and jurisdiction shopping

A lot of company's have operations across the globe. Many of them incorporate themselves or their subsidiaries in certain countries to take advantage of the tax holidays and other investment incentives. There are entire countries in the Caribbean and Europe whose entire GDP is generated from companies not doing business there. This is accounting fraud on a scale that spans the globe. Companies like Google, Apple and Microsoft generate a lot of profits but do not return them to investors. Companies like Apple do not even like to pay dividends. The investor is supposed to take advantage of the rise in stock price and be grateful.

To ensure that the tax man does not take away their profits, these companies use tax-haven-based offshore entities (subsidiary companies registered abroad) that secrete a bulk of the profits. The profits are never returned to home base. The top executives of these companies reward themselves to this money when they go in for their pet mergers and acquisitions. The government does not go after these companies because they have legislators in their pocket.

> 1, 2, 3, 4
> Tech titans escape tax using foreign jurisdictions
> 5, 6, 7, 8
> While the IRS is garnishing wages of ordinary minions

Summary

You may be wondering what college or university teaches such crookedness. Sadly, it is how things are. It is a crooked system that has been built by crooked people over centuries. It is something you learn from reading several books. Visit your local library and spend some time in the non-fiction aisles.

Off-Market Wisdom

- Politics has a huge influence on the markets and the fortunes of individual companies. I believe elections are a sham and that the winners are decided by the globalist kleptocracy. It simplifies a lot of things and helps in making near-accurate predictions about the future.

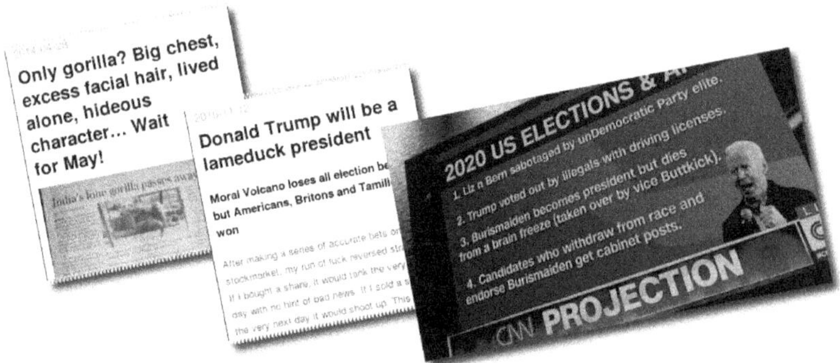

Today, democracy is hamstrung by crony capitalists. They steal power from the people and secure them in the hands of Fascists. (Fascism is corporatism or rule by corporates.) If not for influence-peddling and cronyism, the Reddy brothers would not have grown from nothing to a ₹40,000-crore group. Neither would the Adani group have revenues of over ₹1 lakh crore. As Indira Gandhi said, corruption is universal. If it were not for corruption, would donations to the Clinton foundation dry up after she resigned as Secretary of State?

Never let your politics influence your investment decisions. If BJP is going to come to power and Adani group is going to benefit from it, then invest in those companies ahead of the elections and sell them afterwards. For peace of mind, never go long on companies owned by crony capitalists. You can never tell when their skeletons will be tumbling out.

- *The Economic Times (ET)* is a sister company of *The Times Of India (TOI)* the unassailable leader in paid news. Whenever either paper gushes over something or somebody, fear ominous portends.

When Raghuram Rajan of Chicago Business School was appointed as RBI chairman, the *ET* fell over itself lathering him up. He was a magician who would transform Indian financial industry or so, they said. Later, I found a curious item in the news. Mr. Rajan suggested that Indian government's gold reserves be shipped to the Bank of England to improve 'reserves quality'. (Reuters; July 2014; India central bank seeks to swap gold to improve reserves quality) Apparently, India is such a poor backward nation that it still cannot refine gold to an international delivery standard. Even the 200 tonnes of gold that India bought from IMF in 2013 was just paper gold. No metal reached India. This poor backward nation gave free money to the IMF! (ET; March 2013; Why central banks still go for gold) Later, when Rajan was asked to go by Modi, ET was inconsolable.

```
                    on Mon Jun 20 at 07:11 AM
~/Desktop
$ curl -s -i http://www.financialexpress.com/ | html2text | grep -i -o rajan
 | wc -l
8

                    on Mon Jun 20 at 07:11 AM
~/Desktop
$ curl -s -i http://www.thehindubusinessline.com/ | html2text | grep -i -o r
ajan | wc -l
12

                    on Mon Jun 20 at 07:11 AM
~/Desktop
$ curl -s -i http://www.business-standard.com/ | html2text | grep -i -o raja
n | wc -l
19

                    on Mon Jun 20 at 07:11 AM
~/Desktop
$ curl -s -i http://economictimes.indiatimes.com/ | html2text | grep -i -o r
ajan | wc -l
93
```

I also found ET doing something similar to Arundhati Bhattacharya when she was appointed as SBI chairman... Ms. Bhattacharya is the next best thing after indoor plumbing and the like.

You need to develop your ability to read between lines so that dubious headlines should set your invisible antennae tingling.

SBI will never collect its Maxis telecom loan – Having a female chairman no insurance against corruption – Nothing learned from Kingfisher NPAs

CBI experience in 2G scam shows that Maxis owner is
cut off-bounds for Indian law

These reports from *The Hindu* prove that my subsequent predictions had come true.

SBI posts ₹7,718 crore loss in Q4 due to bond loss, bad loans

This the second consecutive quarter that the lender has made a loss.

May 2018: State Bank of India (SBI), the country's largest lender, posted it's highest ever loss in the fourth quarter — of ₹7,718 crore due to provisions made for losses in its bond portfolio and for bad loans.

...

During the period under review, ₹29,037 crore worth loans slipped into the NPA category, of which ₹17,435 crore was from stressed standard asset category. SBI has classified telecom player Aircel as NPA and has provided 50% of its exposure after the company filed for bankruptcy.

Going ahead, the SBI said it has redefined the segment that lends to large corporates which will now comprise of only AA rated companies.

Banks will pay a price if a telco files for bankruptcy, says SBI

February 2020: SBI Chairman Rajnish Kumar on Saturday said banks will 'have to pay the price' in case any telecom firm files for bankruptcy, a day after the Supreme Court made it clear that telecom companies will have to pay the ₹1.47 lakh crore in past dues.

…

Asked if any telco account is currently classified as non-performing asset (NPA), he said there were two accounts — Aircel and RCom — that went into bankruptcy.

- Rating companies like Moody's and S&P and auditing companies like KPMG and Pricewaterhouse Coopers are considered respectable by the Western press but they were among the prominent ones who enabled the 2008 financial crash. Despite the hundreds of millions they pay in fines, their past involvement in scams and crashes, and their ownership by multi-layered holding companies registered in tax havens, they continue to play a gateway role in Western markets. This is because American politicians have totally defanged the regulators such as **Securities and Exchange Commission (SEC)** and the **Federal Trade Commission (FTC)**. The US industry has a revolving door policy that allows politicians and bureaucrats retire with a golden parachute in the private sector. The Transparency International may rank Western countries higher than Third World countries in terms of least corruption but they turn truth on its head - Western countries are the most corrupt and the United States is the worst because their currencies are costlier than Third World currencies. What Western countries may have done is eliminate low-level corruption but the top is hopelessly corrupt. The families of influence peddlers Hillary Clinton and Joe Biden have made it amply clear that corruption is not racist.

- Satyam Computer Systems was a prominent IT company. Its promoters moved a lot of profitable businesses to a subsidiary company and later wanted to make it totally family-owned. When investors protested, the promoters claimed that the plan was placed before the board at the AGM and approved by most shareholders. Is it any wonder that the group subsequently collapsed as a result of accounting fraud? When a promoter shows his true colours, do not wait around for his company to collapse. Exit the stock as quickly as you can.

- Vijay Mallya's companies were raided several times but no charges were made. If you think they must have paid off the officials, you may be right. It is indicated for a company that does brisk business but does not pay much in dividends.

- World over, government companies have a reputation of being badly run. In India, many of government companies are monopolies and consistently make tons of profit. *Coal India* has a monopoly over Indian coal fields. It is not a glamorous stock but operators buy it up just before it declares its yearly or half-yearly dividend and sell it after collecting the money. This is known as **dividend stripping**. I have remained invested in it to the tune of (₹12,000) despite the price fluctuations. It gives over ₹1000 in dividends each year, which is better than any private company. In case of most private companies, the dividends are already factored in the share price and consequently their **dividend yield** (ratio of dividend to stock price) is not attractive.

- 'Market sentiment' is a huge factor. Before being replaced by tech companies like Infosys and TCS, MNCs of all stripes were considered to be better run than Indian companies. In the 90s, I looked at the stock listing in *The Hindu* and found that the Indian subsidiary of Digital Equipment Corporation (later bought by Compaq, which was in turn bought by Hewlett-Packard) was *undervalued*. I asked my father to invest ₹27,000 in it. He exited it at over ₹70,000.

- In 2016, the Wells Fargo Bank had to fire over 5000 employees after it became known that they had started 2 million accounts without the knowledge of their customers and were charging them fees. Officials right to the top were getting bonuses and raises for doing such a fine job. How can so many people at such a prominent bank be engaged in a such fraudulent activity on such a scale? It ain't true, bro! It must be a conspiracy theory!

- Indians are not allowed to invest in US companies. However, if you are an American, you cannot go wrong with investment in arms manufacturers, can ya? Did you know that the NSA is part of the military?

Pentagon racks up $35 trillion in accounting changes in a year

[deleted]

The Defense Department acknowledged that it failed its first-ever audit in 2018 and then again last year, when it reviewed $2.7 trillion in assets and $2.6 trillion in liabilities. While auditors found no evidence of fraud in the review of finances that Congress required, they flagged a laundry list of problems, including accounting adjustments.

[deleted] This is the textbook definition of accounting fraud!

"In layman's terms, this means that the DoD made adjustments to accounting records without having documentation to support the need or amount for the adjustment," said Dwrena Allen, spokeswoman for the Pentagon's inspector general.

Liberals in the US would be offended if a White person wore a traditional dress from a Third World country (CULTURAL APPROPRIATION!) but if an Obama or a Clinton wants to turn into rubble (HUMANITARIAN BOMBING!), then that is all right with them.

- A lot of brokerage recommendations you read in the media are false. Believing a fool makes you a fool.

Foreign brokerages turn bullish, see Sensex hitting 33K in 6-12 months; top

Edit View History Bookmarks Tools Help

reign brokerages turn bullish, ...

articles.economictimes.indiatimes.com/2015-05-

Readers' opinions (40)

Hiro Bachani (mumbai)
I find it pretty funny. When the markets fall by about 1000 points- many great analysts start predicting that the indian markets will go down to 25,000 and less- but if the markets go up by 1000 points- there are many brokerages who predict that the market will hit 33.000 etc- - who pays these great analysts ? If we were to rely on such advice surely we will be doomed- best is to stick to value investing and fundamentals- and not be swayed by any such arm-chair experts-

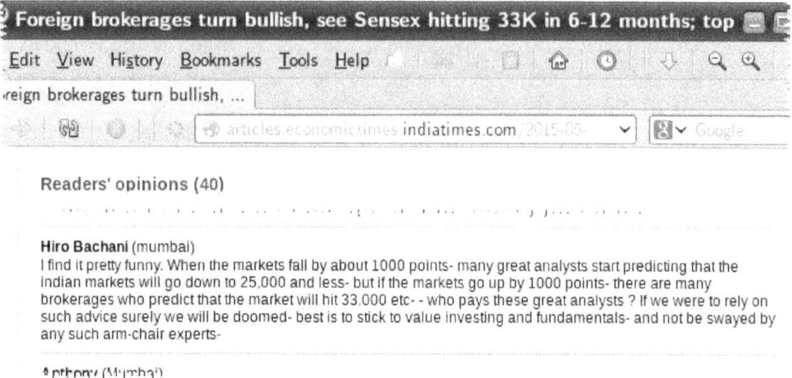

The worst among these fools are foreign brokerages. They make the most bizarre recommendations. I wonder if they have clay in their heads.

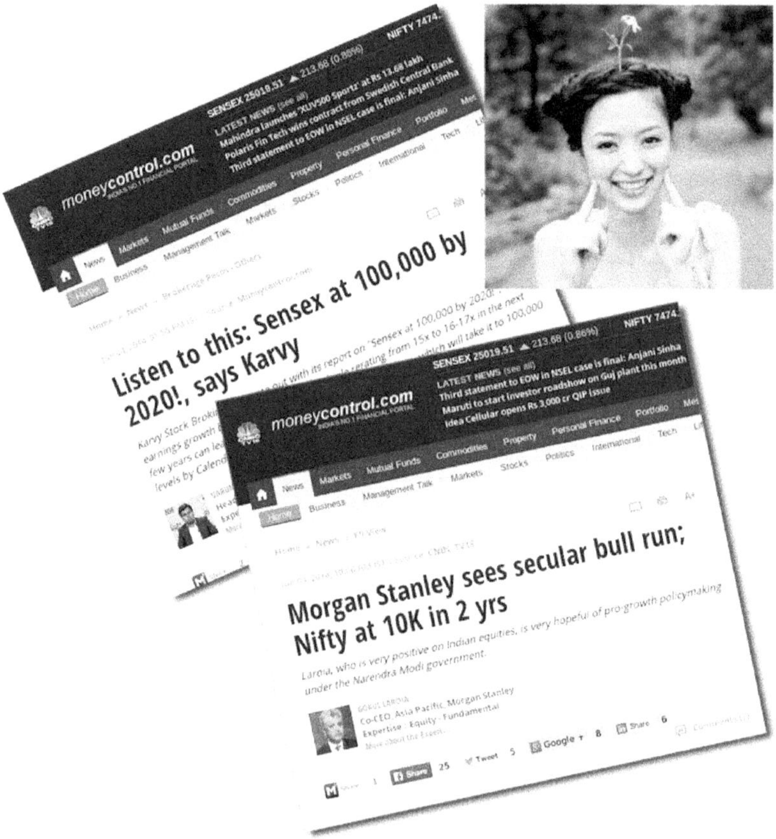

Some brokerage divinations have no basis on market realities. They are politically motivated.

- Some industries have a long gestation period for new projects to come online. The steel industry is an example. My first ever investment in the sharemarket was in the SAIL stock just when it was coming out of a massive restructuring and its price was around ₹5. I sold it at over double the price.

- Reliance Industries Limited's main business is petroleum refining. (Apart from making petrol, diesel, kerosene, naphtha (fuel oil), wax and tar, there is an extensive downstream petrochemicals business. A lot of things we use daily, everything from plastics to detergents, are by-products of the petroleum refining.) The petroleum refining and petrochemicals business is dependent on the price of the crude oil barrel. The higher the price, the greater the margins.

- A notorious bank robber was caught by the police. The police asked him why he robbed banks. He answered, "That's where the money is!" The globalist kleptocracy thinks along the same lines. While there is a lot of money with the people that can be squeezed out of them, the government is a more easier source of unfettered amounts of money. One of the best ways to make money off the government is to start a war or (in sad peacetimes) start white-elephant infrastructure projects. Just search for news headlines for "give war a chance", you will find plenty of articles advocating war because it is a good business. One such devotee of the military-industrial complex, writing in *The New York Times* , had this to say:

> Regarding the sticks, I wouldn't underestimate the impact on a modern European state of sustained NATO air bombardments, which should be intensified once the weather clears. People tend to change their minds and adjust their goals as they see the price they are paying mount. Twelve days of surgical bombing was never going to turn Serbia around. Let's see what 12 weeks of less than surgical bombing does. Give war a chance.

In the case of any white-elephant project, the kleptocracy arranges the loans, contracts the project and then collects the tolls. But both of these money suckers need a lot of taxpayers' money. Because they have already squeezed out all the money from the government in myriad of ways, the kleptocracy wanted the stealing (taxation) to be streamlined. They thought the VAT (value-added tax) could do it. After a lot of trial and error, they have now settled on GST (Goods and Services Tax). Several countries have adopted it or doing so, despite a great deal of opposition. In India, the Modi government passed it in an unconstitutional manner. When the GST debate was going on, the globalists assured India that its sovereign credit would be upgraded if GST was passed. Nothing happened after it did pass. No, sir! It was just a carrot-and-stick policy. When the government asked the rating agencies to upgrade, the agencies let out a collective yawn and murmured something about India's equally yawning fiscal deficit. The Modi government wasted so much for nothing!

- Indian rating agencies like ICRA and CRISIL were originally owned by Indian FIs. Under pressure from the kleptocracy, the Indian government forced them to divest their stakes, which were then picked by the usual suspects Moody's and S&P. Having these corrupt agencies in such a key position is not good for our markets.

- Franklin Templeton is a hallowed name in the mutual funds industry. They are very conservative in their picks and consistent in their returns. But, even they can be had with a dog-and-pony show (the technical name is 'Microsoft Powerpoint presentation'). Six funds run by the Franklin Templeton Mutual Fund (FTMF) in India were recently shut down by SEBI. FT had invested in corporate debt that turned bad. All six Templeton schemes were given good ratings by ratings agencies. Chennai Police is about to register a criminal case against the AMC for attempting to defraud ₹28,000 crores from 3 lakh investors.

FT in India needs a lesson in ethical practices.

- I knew something was seriously wrong when I learned that Franklin Templeton had invested in Ukraine government's bonds. Ukraine was targeted for a regime change by the US and UK. Billions of aid money was spent over a decade to win over politicians, journalists and 'activists'. It all came down to a Russia-friendly democratically elected president being ousted by thugs (or as the Western media called them 'pro-democracy protesters' (including many neo-Nazi groups)) funded by US State Department and a pro-West stooge being placed in his place. An over-confident Ukraine government attacked the industrialised East of the country were ethnic Russians were in a majority. When Russia militarily intervened, it looked as if Ukraine was going to become another failed state under Western tutelage. The 'accidental' downing of a Malaysian plane stopped Russia from further escalation but not before making the Ukraine government bonds worthless. Would a conservative investor like FT invest in such a hotspot if not for pressure from globalists?

- The NSE was started by prominent Indian FIs such as LIC and SBI as a fully automated exchange. It later became de-mutualised (incorporated) and got an independent management. Unlike the BSE, which was run by brokers, the NSE was supposed to be run by professionals. However, key personnel at the top secretly tied up with some brokers to facilitate high-frequency trading using co-located servers. This arrangement gave these brokers an unfair advantage. They could pre-empt the market and make profits, whichever way a stock went.

 ## The fall of NSE: Corruption or hubris?

May 2019, ET: The Securities & Exchange Board of India has penalized NSE Rs. 1,100 crores, and its former chief executives Ravi Narain and Chitra Ramakrishna. The irony of all these is that none of the three playing a key role in building Indian financial markets until yesterday can be a part of it for some period.

Other academic architects who had a hand in the development of Indian stock markets – Ajay Shah and Susan Thomas – the husband and wife duo who could be spotted in the NSE premises often in the '90s stand convicted for stealing data to build algorithm-based trading instead of doing research as claimed.

...

What did NSE and its managers do? For all the transparency it stood for when it came to the outside world, inside it was a cozy club. This is what SEBI had to say: "None of the noticees (NSE, Ravi Narain and Chitra Ramakrishna) have come forward with any explanation as to why they did not have any policy with respect to data sharing nor have they explained as to why Mr. Ajay Shah and Ms. Susan Thomas were being provided with data so generously over the years without signing any agreement with the exchange.

...

It wouldn't be an exaggeration to say that SEBI, NSE and NSDL walked in lockstep to end BSE's dominance. Once the mission was accomplished, the NSE marched on its own probably believing it is above regulations.

...

While one order exhibits the long standing relationship between NSE officials and outside advisers, the other one shows possible negligence and corruption. The exchange is convicted of favouring brokers – Way 2 Wealth, OPG Securities and GKN Securities – who had preferred access to technology. That boosted connectivity and is a clear case of discrimination.

Despite these convictions, the NSE has gone about its way as if nothing had happened. The Ministry of Finance has also done nothing, probably because its officials were aware of what had happened and are hoping the case would disappear from the minds of investors.

- When the NSE became incorporated, some foreign funds invested in the company. After some years, they complained and exited. They were hoping that Indian FIs (that were in effect owned by the government) who started the NSE would divest their stakes. Whenever a stock exchange becomes de-mutualized (incorporated and privatized), corruption sets in. In the US, the Nasdaq (started by the notorious crook Bernie Madoff) is rumoured to be hand-in-hand with some brokerages. Before you can say "Go, man, that sux!", you as an investor should put pressure on the government to clean up the markets.

Q. Where is your main data centre located?
A. We have four data centres in Mumbai, including the one that we launched in October 2015, which is the largest. We have two data centres in Vikhroli. We also have one data centre in the Bombay Stock Exchange building, specifically for algorithmic trading or high frequency trading for brokers. There is a direct fibre connection to the exchange. The latest flagship centre of ours is the one at t

- One of the biggest scandals to come out of the 2008 financial crash was that several Wall Street brokerages routinely bet against their customers. This was illegal then and is illegal now. Somehow, the US government takes no action. If this is not Fascism, then what is?

- Nothing succeeds like success. The news media

⊖ ZeroHedge

"A Gigantic Clusterf**k": How Morgan Stanley Avoided $10BN In Archegos Losses By Selling First

BY TYLER DURDEN   APR 07, 2021 AM

One week ago, in our initial take on the biggest hedge fund collapse since LTCM, we explained that - in our view - the catalyst for the failure of the Archegos hedge fund, which had as much as 10x leverage allowing it to hold some $100BN in positions, was Morgan Stanley and Goldman breaking ranks with their fellow prime brokers, and sparking the biggest margin call since Lehman and AIG.

Turns out we were right.

creates hype about certain individuals. Like mass hysteria, the hype feeds on its success and just becomes ever more hyped up. Even a staid conservative newspaper like *The Hindu* can fall for such hype. This is how crooks develop a larger-than-life persona that obscures their dubious past and precarious present.

- Some news reports may look like they may damage a companies entire business but it may not. Some years ago, a New York newspaper claimed that energy drinks were nothing more than water, sugar and caffeine. This information was not exactly a secret but why rake it up now.

This attack did nothing to dull the sales of Red Bull or its competitors. This is because the success of this drinks is not caffeine or sugar but the sales infrastructure and marketing (and addiction (like tobacco)). One researcher going through the archives of the Coca Cola company found the famous secret recipe of their drink. Even though he published it, it did not affect the sales of the company. Coca Cola is a brand built over several decades with a worldwide sales network. The secret recipe or its associated mythology may have contributed to its early rise but that was all it did.

- Some deep-fisted companies have cronies in the government who are ready to help them even in the face of adverse legal decisions, as Samsung found in its case against Apple. The fact that a newcomer to the mobile space can sue an established leader like Samsung using patents is another reason why should not rush to judgement on the face of bad news.

- Did you know that the famous baby powder made by Johnson & Johnson has nothing special in it for babies? That was not how their ads were claiming. They were lying for all these decades! They have been sued by women who got ovarian cancer after using their talc contaminated with asbestos. Is there nothing in this world that is good and holy these days? If you read the news reports about this case, you will find that the US regulator FDA had been playing hand-in-hand with the J&J in suppressing facts.

- I did not know that private corporations could wage wars until I read the novels of **Jonathan Black**. The first joint-stock outfit **East India Company** not only waged wars but also occupied entire countries and established governments. It was only when I read an American textbook on management (recommended in BBA coursework) that I learned that companies like International Telephone and Telegraph (IT&T) could get the US government to prop up or overthrow foreign governments for them. The heavily censored book by Victor Marchetti *The CIA and the Cult of Intelligence* only reinforced the fact that the US was a Fascist state in

WASHINGTON. AFP: The United States on Saturday took the rare step of vetoing a quasi-judicial trade panel's decision to ban the sale of some Apple products in a blow to rival Samsung.

US Trade Representative Michael Froman announced the move against the International Trade Commission in a letter, saying he decided to "disapprove" the exclusion order.

It is the first time since 1987 that a US presidential administration had vetoed a product ban ordered by the commission.

disguise. (Marchetti was a former employee of the CIA and his passages about the CIA's military support to hostiles in Nagaland shocked me.

Much of it was blacked out but it was clear that the US government was no friend of India. The CIA ran illegal drugs and arms all over the world with the help of the US military and right-wing dictatorships/militias. It even supplied American hookers to foreign countries. The CIA is no friend of any country, not even the United States. The globalist kleptocracy is its only master.)

It is not as if the US Fascists have been very coy about their intentions. After World War I, American Fascists attempted a Fascist coup in the US. In the book *George Bush: An Unauthorized Biography*, I read a curious passage about a 'business plot'.

> Meanwhile, the Warburgs demanded that American Jews not 'agitate' against the Hitler government, or join the organized boycott. The Warburgs' decision was carried out by the American Jewish Committee and the B'nai B'rith, who opposed the boycott as the Nazi military state grew increasingly powerful.
>
> The historical coverup on these events is so tight that virtually the only expose of the Warburgs came in journalist **John L. Spivak's** **"Wall Street's Fascist Conspiracy,"** in the pro-communist *New Masses* periodical (Jan. 29 and Feb. 5, 1934). Spivak pointed out

that the Warburgs controlled the American Jewish Committee, which opposed the anti-Nazi boycott, while their Kuhn Loeb and Co. had underwritten Nazi shipping; and he exposed the financing of pro-fascist political activities by the Warburgs and their partners and allies, many of whom were bigwigs in the American Jewish Committee and B'nai B'rith.

John L. Spivak later underwent a curious transformation, himself joining the coverup. In 1967, he wrote an autobiography (*A Man in His Time*, New York: Horizon Press), which praises the American Jewish Committee. The pro-fascism of the Warburgs does not appear in the book. The former "rebel" Spivak also praises the action arm of the B'nai B'rith, the Anti-Defamation League. Pathetically, he comments favorably that the League has spy files on the American populace which it shares with government agencies.

Thus is history erased; and those decisions, which direct history into one course or another, are lost to the knowledge of the current generation.

I then found Spivak's articles about this 'Wall Street Fasicst conspiracy' and it is true. There was indeed a business plot but it failed take off because Gen. Smedley Butler refused to take part in it.

- The globalist kleptocracy wants an interdependent world. Sovereignty and economic freedom is anathema for them.

Alternative to China? Dear Donald Trump, how about America?

Every country needs its own manufacturing base to protect its sovereignty and to sustain a working class mainstay for the economy.

Stocks Plunge After Trump Vows To Retaliate To China "This Afternoon", Orders US Companies To Find "An Alternative To China"

Our great American companies are hereby ordered to immediately start looking for an alternative to China, including bringing your companies HOME and making your products in the USA. I will be responding to China's Tariffs this afternoon.

Tear up those free-trade accords and leave the WTO. Impose a blanket 20% customs/countervailing duty on all imports. Negotiate individual customs duty arrangements with countries willing to trade with the United States on an equitable basis.

Asking American companies to find an alternative to China is no different than asking them to move to Mexico under NAFTA. America will not be great again unless it returns to manufacturing.

This makes it easy to punish a country when it steps out of line. Every country needs to have its own manufacturing. Offloading important parts of the economy to foreigners will not make your economy stronger. The kleptocrats ridicule any attempt to roll back globalisation as a surrender to 'fissiparous tendencies' but the coronavirus pandemic has proved how precarious the world's superpower was when it ran out of face masks and toilet paper.

The power that China wields on the US government is incomprehensible. When Trump banned travellers from China after the coronavirus was 'discovered' there, US government officials rushed to that country's rescue.

"There is no reason to be walking around with a mask. When you are in the middle of an outbreak wearing a mask might make people feel a little bit better, and it might even block a droplet, it's not providing the perfect protection that people think that it is." - Dr. Anthony Fauci on March 8, 2020.

- After politicians and government officials, it is the media who lie the most to the public. They do so because it is in theirs or others' self-interest. They will do anything to sell the products of their advertisers. The coronavirus pandemic has proved this again and again. Be a sceptic. If they are so ready sell their

'Anti-science saga'? NBC contributor who documented harrowing battle with Covid-19 NEVER had the virus

soul to the highest bidder, why should you believe in anything they say particularly when it does not benefit you.

As it is, the media is full of morons because they have hired immature idiots straight from college where they were brainwashed with Communist propaganda. Just look at their priorities.

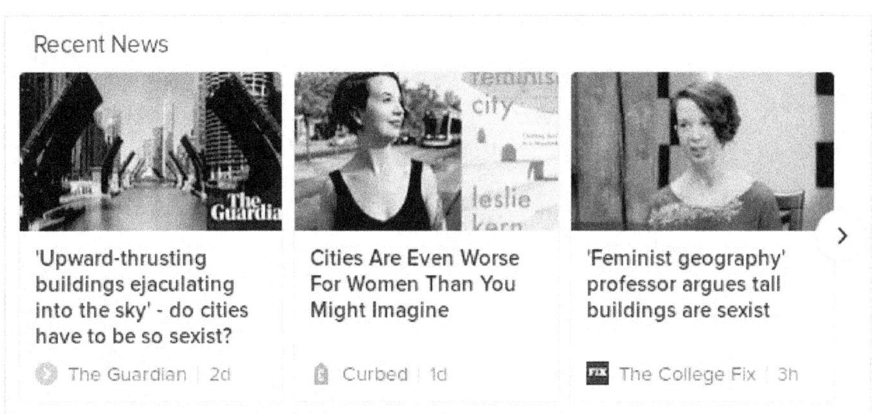

- Tomorrow, Biden will be inaugurated as the US president. What I feared most has not happened… yet. I did not want to jinx things for Trump. There was no reason for Trump to fix what others before him had left irreparably broken. They were so desperate to get back to power that they openly stole the election, just as I predicted one year ago in my editorial/political cartoons book. Well, they can have it. Here are my big predictions for the future. One of them will become true.

  - The US government will default on its debt and devalue its currency. In the name of the 2008 financial crash, wars and now the coronavirus pandemic, the US has printed a lot of currency. This is not going to stop. Several Democrat-run 'blue' states, cities and towns are deep in the red. They are run by traitors who seem to hate

America (thanks to the CommonCore globalist education curriculum) and are blissfully tolerant of anarchists and Communists.

They will need more trillion-dollar bailouts to stay afloat. The bailouts will definitely affect the name and credit of the United States. Foreign countries will not fund its deficit by buying US treasuries. To make foreigners buy the treasuries, the US will have to increase interest rates for foreigners while having it low for Americans. Can it? No. If it devalues its currency, old treasuries will be dumped causing a self-reinforcing spiral to the bottom.

- The US will break up. There is no reason well-run 'red' states fund badly run 'blue' states. The US government will implement police-state tactics to suppress discontent citing some spectacular home-grown 'terrorist' incident(s). An oppressive Federal government will create conditions similar to those that prompted southern states secede before the American Civil War.

- The US will become a prototype police state and force other countries to join it to form a worldwide tyrannical super-state run by globalist kleptocrats.

I think my next book will be a fiction title. May God bless us and rid the world of plutocrats. I wish you the best of luck and fortune.

- If you live in the West, you could try to de-brainwash Communist kids with these coffee-table books.

Tell them that after a Communist revolution succeeds, the educated are the first ones to be executed.

OUR PAGES OF HISTORY

50 years ago: September 5, 1963

World Govt. as only hope for human race

New Delhi, Sept. 4.
Prime Minister Nehru and Earl Attlee today advocated a world Government based on rule of law as the only hope for the survival of the human race and for peace and co-operation among nations.

Mr Nehru and the former Labour Prime Minister, addressing the first All-India World Federalists Conference, emphasised that general disarmament and ending of colonialism and racialism were necessary to achieve such a world order.

Rule of law, as witnessed in Red China

Books By V. Subhash

I started publishing books in 2020 and finished my first year with 21 of them. It must be a record! My first book is one of the biggest jokebooks of all time. My books for children are published under the pseudonym Ólafía L. Óla.

2020 Fresh Clean Jokes For Everyone

This is one of the biggest jokebooks ever written - over 3100 jokes spread over three parts.

- Part 1 (For Learning)
- Part 2 (For Fun)
- Part 3 (For Intellectuals Only)

It has jokes that you don't have to think about - bar jokes, blonde jokes, cross-the-road jokes, knock-knock jokes, lightbulb jokes, pun jokes,... entire chapters for people with special skills or interests - computer jokes, programming jokes, physics jokes, chemistry jokes, biology jokes, medical jokes, financial jokes, geography jokes, knock-knock jokes, romantic (breakup) jokes... for those looking for sharp content, plenty of jokes about philosophy, advertising, news and politics... for kids and students wishing to improve their vocabulary and general knowledge, a treasure house of clever wordplay and interesting facts/riddles, and THREE CHAPTERS DEVOTED TO FOREIGN LANGUAGES. Several funny and thought-provoking poems (mostly as financial/political limericks), set to the tune of popular nursery rhymes. Also, some of the best one-liners EVER written in the English language.

• Pages: 276 • Paperback: $12 • Ebook: An older subset with 420 jokes is available for free.

2020 Fresh Clean Jokes For Kids

This 'for kids' subset of the 2020 jokebook has 2200 jokes. It has all of *Part 1 (For Learning)* and some non-political jokes from *Part 2 (For Fun)* & *Part 3 (Only For Intellectuals)*. Joke types include children's jokes, computer jokes, programming jokes, cross-the-road jokes, physics jokes, chemistry jokes, biology jokes, medical jokes, financial jokes, geography jokes, knock-knock jokes, mix jokes, breakup jokes...). Special chapters include Elephant & Ant Jokes, Off-The-Wall Philosophers, Useful French Phrases, Useful Latin Phrases, Other Useful Foreign Phrases, Jokes You Love To Hate, Jokes In Advertising, and Fancy Creature Jokes.

• Pages: 180 • Paperback: $12 • Ebook: Will never be published

Learn To Ride A Motorcycle In Five Minutes

Of course, you can learn to ride a motorbike in five minutes! For most of my life, I did not know how to ride a motorbike. But, when I had to do, it took me only five minutes. On my first ride on my first bike, I travelled nearly 100 kilometres, across two cities and one national highway. Acquiring the skill takes less than five minutes and honing it will require a few weeks of practice.

• Pages: 40 (30 with real content) • Paperback: $7.70 • Ebook: $3

Vastu Shastra Explained

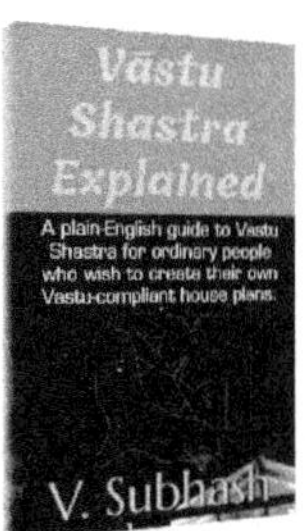

Vastu Shastra Explained is a plain-English Vástu Śastra building-architecture guide for those who wish to draw their own Vastu-compliant house plans. The book does not upsell Vaastu as a panacea for all ills nor does it portray Vastu as the Indian Feng Shui. Instead, it presents Vastu as a collection of time-tested best-practices in Indian building architecture.

The original text of *Vastu Vidya* is available as a free download from my website.

• Pages: 40 (30 with real content) • Colour paperback: $11 • B/W (Grayscale) Paperback: $9 • Ebook: $3

A Really Traditional Alphabet Book

This FULL-COLOUR picture book bundles an alphabet writing-practice book and a jokes-and-puzzles book. It uses the same words that have been traditionally used to teach preschoolers. The jokes and puzzles are for older kids.

• Pages: 34 (32 with real content) • Colour paperback: $7.70

Animalia Humorosum by Ólafía L. Óla

This is an illustrated children's storybook based on Aesop's Fables. The stories have been made more believable by changing the ending with a humorous twist. The book is a large-print full-colour paperback.

• Pages: 30 (26 with real content) • Colour paperback: $12 • Ebook: FREE for parental review

World of Word Ladders by Ólafía L. Óla

A word ladder has a diagram of a ladder with a word on both the first and last rungs. You need to change only one letter in the blank middle rungs so that the first word is transformed into the last word. Your words CANNOT be

- proper nouns,
- abbreviations, or
- loan or slang words.

• Puzzles: 100 • Paperback: $9.90 (one volume) • Ebook: FREE for newsletter subscribers

Olafia L. Ola's Favourite Traditional Nursery Rhymes (Illustrated)

The political correctness pandemic has caused many nursery rhymes to be rewritten or eliminated altogether. This illustrated children's book has **50 popular English nursery rhymes in their traditional form**. The selected rhymes have stood the test of time and this FULL-COLOUR LARGE-PRINT book makes it easy for kids to read them. Bonus content includes a few Aesop's fables, jokes and word ladder puzzles.

• Pages: 44 (38 with real content) • Colour paperback: $11

FFMPEG Quick Hacks

This FULL-COLOUR book provides an extensive FFmpeg tutorial, hack collection and desk-side reference. Quickly learn to use this free command-line video-editing utility - cut, copy, record, edit, tag, convert, rotate, flip, resize, crop, combine, compose, blur, sharpen, smoothen, side-by-side split, PIP inset, fade in/out... Also learn to use subtitles, audio/image files and metadata with video.

• Pages: 152 • Colour paperback: $36 • Ebook: FREE or $1.99

CommonMark Ready Reference

MarkDown is an easy human-readable text format that can serve as the common base for exporting to multiple document formats such as HTML, ODF, DOC/DOCX, PDF and ebook (EPUB, MOBI...). It is a great tool for authors, technical writers and content developers to create books, manuals, web pages and other rich-text content. CommonMark is a new well-formed standard for the old MarkDown spec. **CommonMark was one of the reasons I was able to write and design 21 books in one year.** Incidentally, this is the first-ever book on CommonMark. You will be buying a piece of history! This book's covers are designed like a quick reference card - free PDF download also available.

• Pages: 60 (42 with real content) • Paperback: $7.70 • Ebook: $3

Email Newsletter Strategies For Profit

An organically grown mailing list is an invaluable resource for your business. It is your own social network. You need to nurture it like a baby. This book not only explains how to create user-friendly email newsletters but also helps you improve email deliverability, organically grow your mailing list, implement industry-standard best-practices and apply practical troubleshooting tips and tricks.

• Pages: 40 (33 with real content) • Paperback: $7.70 • Ebook: $3

Linux Command-Line Tips & Tricks

Because of its ancient history, BASH scripting has some odd programming constructs that are difficult to memorize. This book tries to provide a ready-reference for such archaic but crucial details. It does not teach you the basics or try to be a comprehensive reference. It focuses on things you are most likely to forget. It is also a great tips-and-tricks collection for Linux command-line warriors.

• Pages: 78 • Paperback: $7.70 • Ebook: $3

Cool Electronic Projects

If you are learning electronics or thinking of it as a future hobby, here are some fun home-improvement projects to begin with. These DIY electronic circuits will be extremely useful (particularly in emergencies), are quite easy to make and will not waste your time or money. Just one of these projects uses AC (alternating current). The rest work on DC (direct current) and are safe for kids (if you think soldering is safe). These projects are good for the environment too, as they reuse electronic parts that would have been discarded. If you are a prepper or survivalist, then you will be happy that all the projects will run off-the-grid, as they can consume renewable energy. For the tinkerer, there are projects that add MORE POWER than what the manufacturer had designed for. For the parent of lazy children, there are annoying alarms that can wake up the dead. The circuit designs are explained in plain English. No exotic projects or obscure concepts. Simple and straightforward.

• Pages: 40 (33 with real content) • Colour paperback: $12 • Ebook: $3

How To Invest In Stocks, 2nd Ed.

The first edition of this book was written (in 2003) for the Indian stockmarket. It was popular around the world as it was a plain-English guide to investing in the stockmarket. It assumed that you do not know anything about stocks, company law, finance or commerce. This completely revised second edition maintains this original USP but has a global focus, updated information and new chapters. **It has some useful 'extra' information that you will not find in any investment book and no business school will teach you.**

• Pages: 94 • Paperback: $9 • Ebook: $3

Dictionary Of Indian English

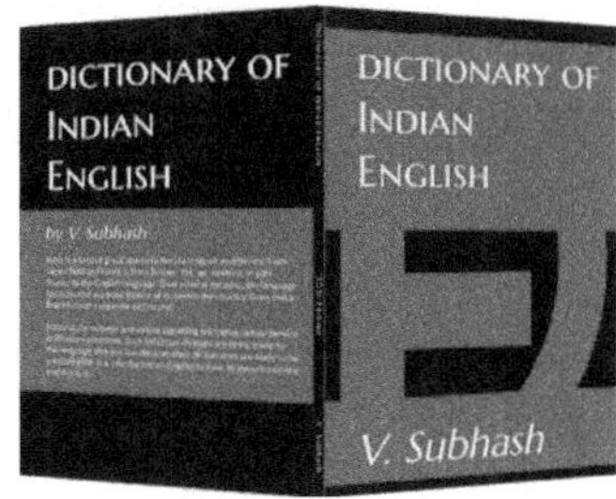

India is a land of great diversity. Kerala is about as different from Tamil Nadu as France is from Britain. Yet, we move on, in part thanks to the English language. English has acquired a unique flavour of its own in the country that we find that even Oxford dictionary is wrong in the Indian context. And, there are words that are unique to India, such as "prepone," which are not used anywhere else. In the first edition, this Dictionary of Indian English (DoIE) provide a ready reference for around 400 such words and phrases. In a future edition, it will become a full-fledged dictionary. Its time will come because of the fast-spreading pandemic of political correctness and mass stupidity.

• Pages: 36 (26 with real content) • Paperback: $7.70 • Ebook: $3

The Devil's Dictionary (Illustrated)

This book makes a fantastic gag gift!

The Devil's Dictionary by Ambrose Bierce from 1911 is a great repository of brutally frank and unusually cynical descriptions for popular words and phrases in English. In my 2020 remake, the original text has been illustrated with contemporary caricatures (of Alexandria Ocasio Cortez, Bill Gates, Don Lemon, Elon Musk, Joe Biden...). It has the **neat easy-on-the-eye look of any new dictionary (modern fonts, two-column pages, starting/ending words on every page).**

If you consider yourself as a woke, liberal, Leftie, Progressive, Socialist, Communist, Feminist... then this book is not for you. This book by Bierce is a product of its time and may not match your unrealistic expectations.

• Pages: 160 • Paperback: $9 • Ebook: $3

How To Install Solar

This is a heavily illustrated 2021 guidebook for **INDIAN** solar power enthusiasts, DIY hacks, home-owners and electricians about solar panels, batteries, inverters, charge controllers, installation procedures and costs. It starts with a simple introduction to home electrical systems, proceeds on to describe various aspects of solar power and options available for home owners, and then provides step-by-step instructions for installing a low-cost DC-only solar charge controller system for ₹6000 and a solar inverter system providing AC power backup for ₹30,000. Also included is an extensive FAQs section based on questions and reviews published by solar power users online.

• Pages: 75 • Colour paperback: £7.70 • Ebook: ₹120

Other books not identified here

- The funniest book ever (by quality) with 149 political/satirical cartoons and commentary (mostly about USA and India) spread over 432 pages. Here is some praise that the book had received:
    - **Hillary Clinton**
      "This is pure Indian propaganda!"
    - **New York Times**
      "This book is full of lies, mostly sourced from our newspaper and other mainstream media outlets."
    - **CNN**
      "This book may have more fake news than CNN but it is not the quantity that matters."
- Two volumes of humorous tweets by a deceased Communist mass-murderer from the East.

• These details are subject to change. • The book images are not actual photos. • I have published some books under pseudonyms. • Latest information, discounted purchase options, advance review copies (ARCs) and full/sample PDF ebooks are available at **www.VSubhash.in**. Apart from books, I also publish feature articles, blog posts, server/desktop software and mobile apps on the site.